# ROCKET INTO DIGITAL

## THE ART OF **DIGITAL MARKETING** AND **SOCIAL MEDIA** FOR SMALL BUSINESSES

Vincent Wee

Rocket Into Digital

Written and edited by Vincent Wee
Cover design by Vincent Wee

Copyright © 2016 by Vincent Wee. All rights reserved.

Disclaimer: While every attempt has been made to verify the accuracy of information in this book as it goes to press, the authors and publisher cannot guarantee its future accuracy. Please consult competent expert advice before taking decisions in response to the advice herein.

All rights reserved. No part of this publication may be reproduced or transmitted in any form or by any means, electronic of mechanical, including photocopying, recording, or use in an information storage or retrieval system, without prior written permission from the author. Any person who does any unauthorized act in relation to this publication may be liable to criminal prosecution and civil claims for damages.

Visit my website: http://www.VincentWee.com/

Printed in the United States of America

First Edition: August 2016

Special Thanks: Elgena Lim

# Table of Contents

| | |
|---|---|
| Preface | 7 |
| Introduction | 9 |
| | |
| **Chapter 1: How Digital Marketing is the Midas Touch for Small Business** | **11** |
| Moving from Traditional to Digital Marketing Platforms | 12 |
| Customer Behaviour with Digital Marketing | 13 |
| Small Business Spending on Digital Marketing | 15 |
| The Reach of Digital Marketing | 16 |
| | |
| **Chapter 2: Experiential Marketing vs. Interactive Marketing** | **21** |
| Experiential Marketing for Small Businesses | 21 |
| Interactive Marketing for Small Businesses | 24 |
| Why Interactive Marketing Wins | 27 |
| | |
| **Chapter 3: More than Facebook: Understanding SEO and Digital Trends** | **33** |
| Facebook as a Digital Marketing Tool | 33 |
| Search Engine Optimization (SEO) | 35 |
|     Tips: Quick Tips on SEO | 39 |
| Digital Trends | 42 |
|     Tips: Quick Tips on Analytics | 49 |
| | |
| **Chapter 4: Making the Most from Google** | **53** |
| Google AdWords | 55 |

| | |
|---|---|
| Tips: Quick Tips on Google AdWords | 58 |
| Google Display Network (GDN) | 60 |
| Remarketing | 62 |

## Chapter 5: Build the Brand by Maximizing Social Media Presence — 65

| | |
|---|---|
| Facebook | 66 |
| Tips: Quick Tips on Facebook | 69 |
| Twitter | 71 |
| Instagram and Pinterest | 73 |
| LinkedIn | 75 |
| Social Media Marketing Tips for Brand Building | 78 |

## Chapter 6: Why Going Digital can Triple Sales Growth — 83

| | |
|---|---|
| Multi-channel Digital Platforms | 84 |
| Retargeting (Remarketing Revisited) | 86 |
| Convenience | 87 |
| Case Study: The Changing Music Industry | 88 |
| Case Study: Cross-Channel Marketing Drives Digital Sales | 91 |
| What Is In It For Small Businesses? | 93 |

## Chapter 7: Rounding up Digital Marketing Components — 97

| | |
|---|---|
| The Website | 97 |
| Search Engine Optimization (SEO) | 100 |
| Search Engine Marketing (SEM) | 101 |
| Social Media | 102 |
| Email Marketing | 104 |
| Content Marketing | 107 |
| Tips: A to Z of Content Marketing | 109 |
| Video Marketing | 112 |

Mobile Marketing 113

**Chapter 8: Gaining the Vivid Competitive Edge** 117
Build 117
Evolve 118
Learn 118
Participate 119
Giveaway 120
Interact 120
Spread 121
Visibility 121
Focus 122

**Chapter 9: Bridging the Distance Gap and Maintaining Customer Closeness** 127
Discerning Customer Perceptions and Identifying their Needs 128
Integrating Digital Marketing Channels 129
Digital Marketing Should Make a Difference 129
Engage the Customer 130
Business Transparency 130
Being Accountable 131
Social Responsibility 132
Build a Personal Relationship 132

**Conclusion** 137
**About the Author** 141

**Rocket Into Digital**

# Preface

The only thing that remains constant in business is change, and this is particularly the case when it comes to marketing techniques. This book has come about as small businesses are shifting their marketing strategies from conventional methods to more modern digital platforms. There seems to be a disconnect, however, between what small businesses believe digital marketing is, and what it entails for the development and growth of their businesses.

Mastering Digital Marketing and Social Media as an art is essential for small businesses who have only been using these tools as a means to an end. This book has all the practical information that you, as a small business marketer, will need to propel yourself into the digital marketing world. Even better, your presence using these strategies should result in more customers, higher profits, and a stronger brand (if done right). This book will explain how to do all of these things, the right way.

**Rocket Into Digital**

# Introduction

Small businesses face big challenges, one of which is in being able to market their products or services. When faced with competition from large enterprises, it seems almost impossible to compete effectively. Large businesses have the benefit of massive budgets, allowing them to take advantage of a whole range of advertising channels.

They also tend to capitalize on traditional marketing channels, which include television advertising, radio advertising and print media (including billboards and newspaper adverts). These are effective, but they are also expensive. For there to be an adequate effect on customers, advertising needs to be in a 'campaign' mode.

Small businesses, however, can compete by taking a different approach. In light of their challenges, including minimal budgets, a lack of technical expertise, and powerful competitions, these businesses are opting for digital marketing platforms to reach their customers.

Digital marketing allows small businesses to compete effectively using their wits. This type of marketing ensures that customers can interact directly with the business, allowing for relationship building to guarantee customer satisfaction. Small businesses are also able to take advantage of their creativity, by creating online digital marketing campaigns that can turn viral, meaning that their marketing messages are repeatedly and enthusiastically shared with many people online.

Despite this fact, small businesses today still face some challenges when it comes to discerning digital marketing and social media. They know about it, they have a general idea of what should be done, but they are unable to create campaigns that will improve their bottom line.

This book seeks to elaborate on the strategies that a business can take to rocket effectively into digital, and fully understand the art and science of using digital marketing techniques and social media platforms. Understanding how to use these tools can lead to building increased sales and customer loyalty. For a small business, a loyal customer is a lifeline because, as long as the client keeps coming back, the business has a good chance of survival and growth.

Digital marketing is the only way forward for any business that is looking to grow and succeed in today's competitive climate. It is imperative that businesses are able to best utilize the tools that are available to them so that they can make the most of the digital opportunities.

This book is designed to be the supporting guide for any small business, a great tool to refer to when embarking on any digital campaign.

# Chapter 1

## How Digital Marketing is the Midas Touch for Small Business

The Midas touch refers to a Greek Myth where a king named Midas had the ability to turn everything that he touched into gold. Considering the value of gold in olden times, and even today, the power to transform something invaluable into something valuable beyond measure creates an excellent opportunity for small businesses.

*Myth of King Midas*

## Rocket Into Digital

A little less than a decade ago, small businesses had marketing strategies that capitalized on tried and tested traditional marketing methodologies. If one wanted to reach their consumers, they made sure that they were listed in the yellow pages, had advertisements in the classifieds, gave out flyers at busy shopping centers and occasionally invested in radio advertising, television adverts and features in magazines. This was fine in those days, but today, times have definitely changed.

## Moving from Traditional to Digital Marketing Platforms

Consumers today are moving away from traditional media and communication, and living in a more digitalized world. Rather than rushing to the newspaper stand when a person wants to find out the latest news, they are more likely to log onto a news website, or use a search tool to check out a headline. To listen to the latest music, rather than tune into the radio, they will log on to YouTube and watch the music video, find a website that is streaming live music, or they could even opt to pay for a download of an entire album in seconds. Rather than watching television adverts, consumers choose to flip through channels so that they can get a feel of what other programs are available. The changing consumer behavior has inevitably led to a change in the marketing tools being used.

This behavioral change can be noticed when one takes note of how modern consumers are browsing for information or working online. This change affects the way that the marketing messages should be delivered to consumers, as well as the medium that should be used. Most web pages have a host of flashing advertisements with 'click-bait' headlines to prompt customers to take a particular call-to-action.

There has been evidence to suggest that consumers will often block out traditional marketing messages on billboards, signs and banners. On the other hand, digitally, they are tempted to interact and in fact 'click' on the advert for more information or to purchase a product/service.

## Customer Behavior with Digital Marketing

Small businesses have begun to realize how this behavior presents an excellent opportunity for interaction with their customers. The biggest advantage that this behavior has provided is higher conversion rates for their clientele. A conversion rate is basically how many customers will respond positively with a sale or decisive action, as a result of viewing an advertisement.

In traditional marketing, it is extremely difficult to gauge whether consumers have been led to a purchase based on a billboard or magazine advertisement. What can be estimated is how many people have been exposed to the marketing communication, and an estimate can be given as to their demographic. With digital marketing, however, one can evaluate how many people have viewed an advertisement, how many clicked on the advert, and finally, how many people were driven to make a purchase. In addition to this information, it is also possible to evaluate whether those who have been driven to action fit within the required demographics.

Digital marketing has given small businesses these golden opportunities. By having more focused advertisements guaranteed to reach the right demographics (and other relevant people that may be interested in the products or services), it becomes much easier to get people to make a purchase.

## Rocket Into Digital

Another advantage of digital marketing is that the process of seeing the advert, and making a purchase, are significantly shortened. This is because, with a few simple clicks, a person can make a purchase online. Traditional marketing requires the customer to locate a shop or outlet before a purchase can be made.

*Google Display Banners on CNET with Call-To-Actions*

In the past, small businesses would have to include coercion in their communication to get people to use their shops or stores to complete a transaction. With digital marketing tools, it is easier to not only convince a client to make a purchase, but to finish that purchase within minutes using online payment platforms. Rather than convincing a customer to make a purchase, as is the case in traditional marketing, digital marketing tries to facilitate the transaction, making it easy for a customer to make and carry out a purchase decision.

## Small Business Spending on Digital Marketing

As more customers are reacting positively to digital marketing techniques, the budget being spent on digital marketing as a whole is more significant than that of traditional media. Therefore, it can be concluded that a higher percentage of the overall marketing budget would probably be spent on digital marketing in the near future. The reason for this spending shift is simple: digital marketing is much cheaper than traditional forms of marketing.

## Digital advertising spending worldwide from 2012 to 2018 (in billion U.S. dollars)

This statistic contains data on the worldwide digital advertising expenditure in 2012 and 2013 with a forecast until 2018. The source projected that global digital ad spending would reach 252.02 billion U.S. dollars by 2018.

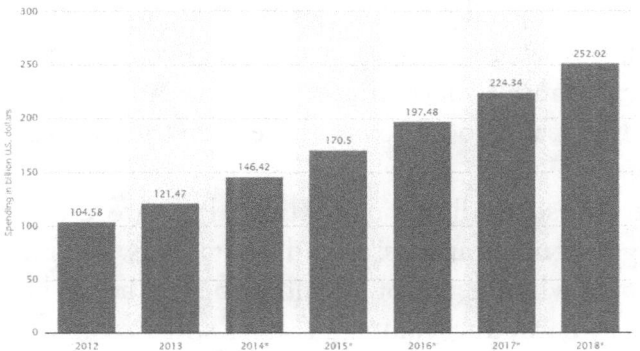

*Source: www.statista.com*

Small businesses are always likely to face a challenge with their budgets, especially when it comes to allocation of their budget towards marketing. They must market effectively to grow their businesses and the cost of a television or newspaper campaign can be extremely high for most small businesses. Therefore, effectiveness is extremely important, and digital marketing allows for targeting, which means that the right audience is being targeted for every marketing campaign. This targeted marketing strategy increases the conversion rate, as the right message will be communicated across to the right audience.

Small businesses can also measure their return on investment (ROI) with digital marketing. Technology allows them to measure the cost per lead of all adverts, and, therefore, see how much revenue they make for every cent that is spent. This makes it easier to make quick decisions on altering campaigns or capitalizing on a campaign that is going well.

That said, on a digital marketing campaign, a small business can choose to spend anywhere from a few cents a day, to hundreds of dollars on each day. This is important for small businesses that may not have established a steady stream of revenue yet. Digital marketing allows for flexible budgeting strategy and payments, therefore, during hard financial times, a small business can pause a marketing campaign, and when times pick up again, they can choose to continue with the campaign.

There are also some digital marketing platforms that allow free marketing for small businesses and individuals. Therefore, even during times when it is not possible for the small business to spend on a marketing campaign, it is still possible to ensure that their marketing message is reaching some consumers.

## The Reach of Digital Marketing

Digital marketing is available on more platforms than

computers or laptops. One can market digitally to people using cellular phones and mobile devices as well. This significantly increases power and reach, getting consumers to interact with products and begin to make purchases. No other media is able to reach customers so conveniently, and so thoroughly become a part of their day to day lives. Most people will spend several hours a day on their mobile devices, and therefore the power of digital marketing should not be underestimated.

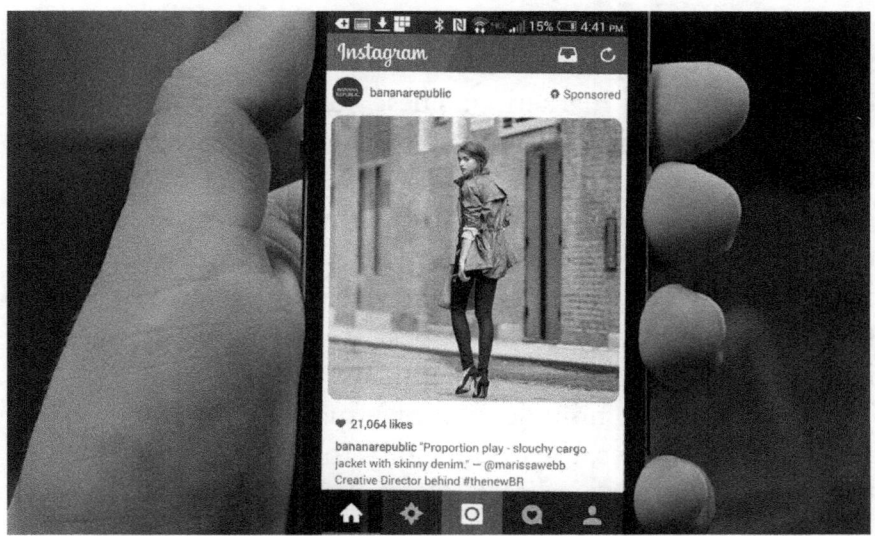

*Instagram Ads on Mobile*

Digital marketing also offers another golden opportunity for businesses that are seeking to create and maintain a competitive edge. This is particularly true for small businesses, as many of them have been slow on the uptake when it comes to digital marketing. By having a presence online, small businesses are able to substantially increase their company reach, giving them access to the international market at a marginal cost. This allows them to compete with big companies, and if they have very creative campaigns, they can even surpass the marketing outcome of those big companies.

This is particularly important for small businesses that may be operating within local markets that are already saturated. In this type of market, it becomes very challenging to find new customers, which also makes it difficult for the company to grow. Access to an international market will break invisible barriers and helps businesses to flourish.

Small businesses are also able to take advantage of multiple channels of digital marketing. These channels include, but are not limited to: email messaging, instant messaging or chats, mobile marketing, the internet (ad extensions and AdWords), social media marketing (hashtags), and video marketing. As digital marketing continues to grow, all of these channels increase or decrease in regards to their importance and use. Currently, the platforms that appear to be gaining momentum include the video marketing platforms and mobile marketing. These allow for communication of visual and direct messages. For small businesses, the opportunity to reach their consumers through direct or indirect channels leads to heightened effectiveness.

"Innovation needs to be part of your culture. Consumers are transforming faster than we are, and if we don't catch up, we're in trouble."

- Ian Schafer (CEO, Deep Focus)

**Rocket Into Digital**

# Chapter 2

# Experiential Marketing vs. Interactive Marketing

Small businesses have a disadvantage when it comes to marketing, especially when they are faced with aggressive large companies that are in the same field. That disadvantage is the budget that is available for marketing campaigns. By being small, the budgets of small businesses are also diminutive, and, therefore, small businesses have to come up with ways that they can capitalize and get the most out of a small budget.

**Experiential Marketing for Small Businesses**

Experiential marketing as a strategy has been a perfect and practical solution. Experiential marketing sometimes called "engagement marketing", "on-ground marketing" or "participation marketing", is a marketing strategy that directly engages consumers and encourages them to participate in the evolution of a brand. It is a form of guerrilla marketing, which aims to get the clients to experience the product, and by doing so, purchase the product.

In addition to promoting an experience of the product,

experiential marketing is also concerned with giving a message about the product, the kind of message that goes beyond the generic and creates a deep association in the mind of the consumer. The messages that are used in experiential marketing campaigns are thought provoking, interesting and quite occasionally, doused with a healthy sense of humor. The result is creating a memory for the consumer that they can always refer to, and, in this way, lay the building blocks for customer loyalty.

Small businesses use these type of campaigns for various reasons. The foremost reason is these campaigns are highly affordable. The primary cost of coming up with these campaigns is in creativity, and this does not require hiring a marketing agency, it requires research, passion and attentiveness to detail. Although this may seem that the small business must hire a specialist or someone with a creative skill set, all that is actually needed is someone who can look for and manipulate ideas.

The second reason is that experiential campaigns allow for direct interaction with the customers. This makes it easier to get feedback on the effectiveness of the campaign, and to understand what the customer likes or does not like about the product or service. It also allows the small business manager to see, first-hand, how a consumer reacts to a product or service. It allows a small business marketer to create buzz and excitement around the product so that the customer is determined to give it a try.

The third reason is that these campaigns are highly flexible, in that they can be changed on a whim due to their inexpensive nature. This means that small businesses can find ways to capitalize on their marketing campaigns, to ensure that they get the customers that they need every time they participate in a campaign. If they are targeting varying demographics or locations for their customers, the ability to change the execution method of a campaign can lead to stronger associations and connections between the customer and the small business.

*Experiential Marketing in Changi Airport (Singapore)*

A review of experiential marketing will reveal that it falls under a traditional marketing technique, particularly because of the channels that are used to reach the customers. These channels are not digital: they are mainly physical channels that require a customer to sample or test a product, or they are subliminal messages placed on signage and print mediums.

## Interactive Marketing for Small Businesses

Interactive marketing, on the other hand, is what one will find when reviewing a digital platform. This is a strategy that is used in digital marketing. Small businesses are translating their traditional guerrilla marketing tactics and placing them online, on interactive platforms. This type of marketing calls the clients to action and gets them to purchase or try a product in the same way that experiential marketing would. In a way, this type of marketing is changing digital messages from a one-sided type of interaction, to one that is more conversational and two-sided.

Interactive marketing entails coming up with creative ways to get a customer to try a product or pay attention to an advertisement. Like traditional marketing, the internet is flooded with advertisements that pop up on virtually every web page that a person will interact with. These advertisements can have two effects on customers: they may opt to click on the ads to find out more or make a purchase, or, they could completely block them out. For small businesses, this creates a better online experience, rather than providing necessary information to clientele.

Small businesses that use interactive marketing online have understood something essential about their customers. Online platforms tend to look at customers as numbers, a mass market where the aim is to get as many clicks as possible and push these to translate into sales. The customer may feel like they are a simple demographic, and that their value is diminished.

By offering interactive marketing to customers, it reveals that the business is interested in building a relationship with the customer, and that each and every customer is an important individual whose business is valued. This is one reason that many people will opt to work with a small business rather than a larger one: the feeling that they can get something customized to cater to their particular need, and that the business cares enough to do it.

*Lightsaber Escape by Google for Star Wars: The Force Awakens*

Creating the interactive experience online is quite straightforward. An example is personalizing a website for the customer so that when they log in, they see a welcome message, and their name displayed somewhere on the web page. This creates a positive user experience (UX). A good user experience is one which is pleasurable, thoughtfully crafted, makes consumers happy, and gets them immersed. When websites save the profile information for their customers, they can send them targeted advertisements that cater to their specific interests as well as encourage eventual sales.

## Rocket Into Digital

For the customer, interactive marketing allows them to provide their feedback openly to a small business. While, on social platforms, customers are able to create posts or leave comments about the product or service that they have used. They are also able to receive immediate responses to any of their queries. In essence, interactive marketing pulls the customer into the experience of a brand, allowing them to view the brand online, as they would if they were visiting a physical location.

*Traveler Reviews on Agoda*

Word of mouth is powerful, especially on the internet. A customer who has had an excellent experience interacting with a small business online could leave a review, mention something on their social networking site, send out emails or even upload a positive review video. As customers rely on each other's opinions more than those of an organization, the result will be increased confidence in the business by the general public, and a high possibility that this will translate into new sales.

Interactive marketing is fun, and can include games, websites, videos, and so on. It could tell a story, personalize an

## Experiential Marketing vs. Interactive Marketing

advertisement, take advantage of multimedia technology, or give an excellent offer. This type of marketing is good for small businesses, as they can assess the effectiveness of their advertisements easily, and make changes where necessary to attract new clientele when they need them.

*Get Peanutized allows users to transform themselves into a 'Peanuts' character*

## Why Interactive Marketing Wins

Experiential marketing has excellent advantages, but it has some disadvantages, as well. The first disadvantage is in the customer reach. Yes, it allows for close interaction with the customer, but the customer must come to the location of the marketing campaign, or the campaign must be based in an area where the target market can be found. This means that on a given day, the campaign can possibly reach a few hundred people, and from this, a good result would be a conversion rate of around 25%.

This disadvantage of experiential marketing translates into a significant advantage for interactive marketing. As interactive marketing is carried out on a digital platform, it is possible to reach hundreds of thousands of potential customers through every single campaign. This is excellent news for small businesses, as it reflects a cost saving that they could not have considered before. Mass marketing by large companies is done through print and television campaigns, and small businesses can now enjoy the same advantages at a fraction of the expense.

Experiential marketing can also backfire if it is carried out without the adequate amount of creativity. It is most effective when people can be engaged, but if the message or activation is lackluster, it can have detrimental effects on the business, and lead to the loss of customers. For a small business, anything that costs them their reputation should be avoided, as this can lead to long-term damage or even closure.

Interactive marketing is becoming easier and easier, as more online tools are available for the purpose of interacting with customers. There is also the added benefit of quick research to find out the best ways to build a two-way relationship with customers. In fact, when developing a website today, the main options include a platform for customers to interact with the business, by having live chats, testimonial pages, forums, and comment sections on blogs. As these are available in templated formats, it makes it easier for a small business manager to implement a successful campaign, even though they may not have a significant amount of technical knowledge.

Experiential marketing campaigns require a massive amount of man hours for there to be measurable results. With this, there is the added cost element that sneaks in, as an activation team is often required. For the campaign to be successful, this team has

## Experiential Marketing vs. Interactive Marketing

to include people with some marketing and communication skills, which further adds to the cost of the campaigns.

Interactive marketing campaigns do not require massive manpower. Usually, a skilled developer and perhaps an enthusiastic marketer are all that is required. With these, messages can be designed and sent out to the right customers. An even bigger advantage here is the element of cost, which is diminished with digital options such as pay per click and pay per view, where the small business only makes payment if a potential client actually interacts with, or clicks on an advertisement on a website. This is of great advantage to small businesses who need their marketing campaigns to directly result in a positive revenue.

**Rocket Into Digital**

"Uber is efficiency with elegance on top. That's why I buy an iPhone instead of an average cell phone, why I go to a nice restaurant and pay a little bit more. It's for the experience."

- Travis Kalanick (Founder, Uber)

**Rocket Into Digital**

# Chapter 3

# More than Facebook: Understanding SEO and Digital Trends

Large businesses can afford to have entire marketing and information technology (IT) departments that are dedicated to creating and executing marketing campaigns, both on traditional platforms and digital ones. Small businesses, however, do not have the capacity for this in most cases, and they have more of a 'test the waters' approach when it comes to digital marketing.

**Facebook as a Digital Marketing Tool**

When creating messages for the online platform, one of the first tools that comes to mind is to capitalize on social media. One of the most popular social media networks in the world is Facebook, which has more than half a billion members from all over the world.

Facebook has also perfected the art of targeted marketing for the online customer. Through information that they collect from Facebook member profiles, they can ensure the adverts that appear on Facebook timelines are relevant to the likes and interests of the person.

When creating an advertisement for Facebook, some criteria allow an individual to narrow exactly who they want to approach, based on their demographic information, interests, skills and even their career placement. For small businesses, this is often the first route that is taken when venturing into digital marketing. The advantages that drive small businesses to this strategy include the low cost of marketing. These Facebook ads only charge when a customer clicks on a link, where he/she will be brought to a landing page, or when he/she views a sponsored post where marketing messages are communicated. Further, the popularity of Facebook as a social media network is a reassurance to the small business owner that it is possible to find all the necessary clientele to market to on this site.

*Advertisements on Facebook*

Although this strategy for advertising does have its benefits, small business owners and managers need to broaden their focus and experience the other digital marketing tools that exist. Focusing on a singular tool means that they are missing out on other opportunities that can positively affect their profitability.

The first important tool that every small business should utilize is Search Engine Optimization, also known as SEO.

## Search Engine Optimization (SEO)

In the past, when someone wanted to find business information using a directory, they would turn to the yellow pages and let their fingers do the walking. This exhaustive method provided information on businesses. With the advent of technology, a new digital yellow pages has been created, and that is the search engine.

A search engine allows a person to look for information about a website. Search engines can find information for an area, a country, or even the whole globe, and present this information in list form based on keyword relevance. A search engine helps consumers to connect with businesses while online.

At the very least, every business, whether large or small, should have a website. A website is an important point of interaction for the customer, and can be referred to as the online office for the business. It is the website that a customer will refer to when they are looking for information about a product or service, when they want to find out the physical location of the business, are looking for a quick shopping solution or they need to get in contact with a company. A website should be the basis of any digital marketing process.

The measure of the effectiveness of a website is how many

# Rocket Into Digital

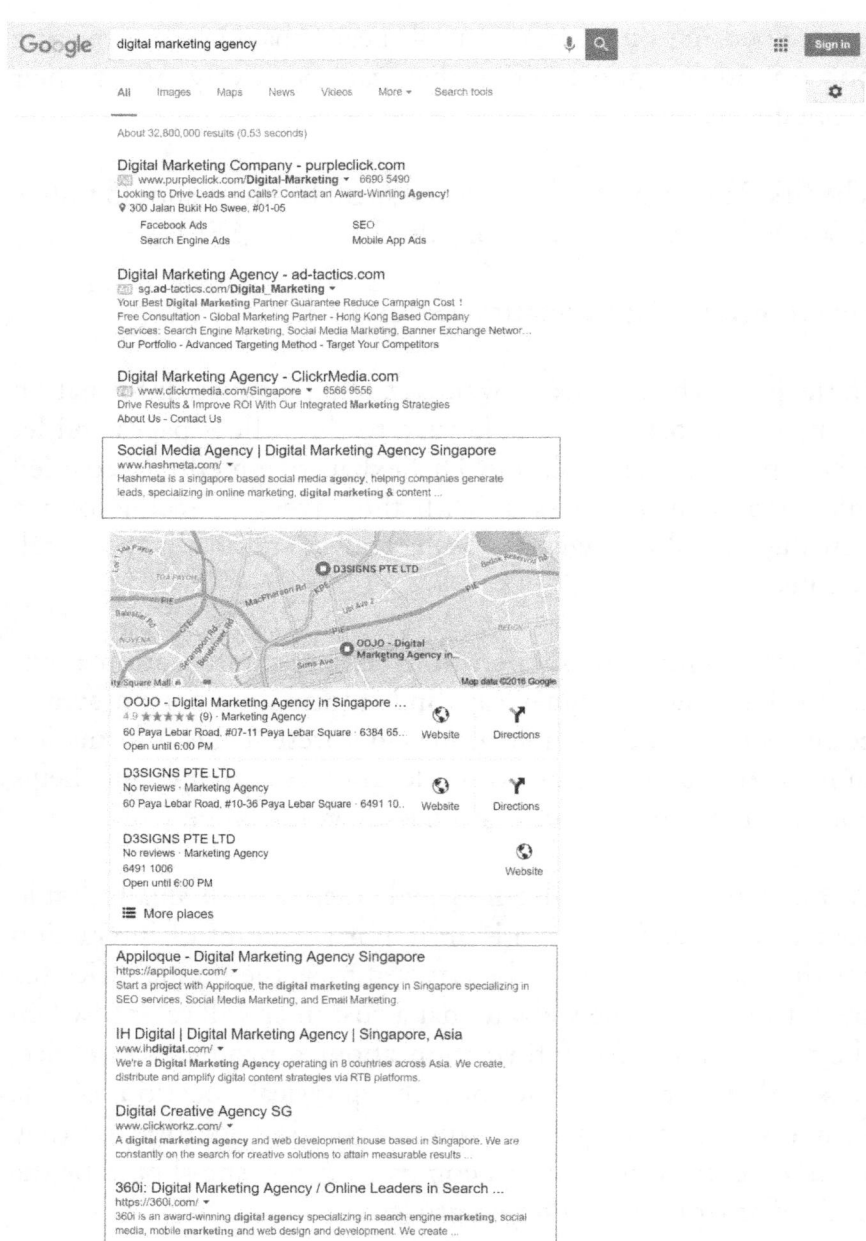

*Search Results on Google*

'clicks' it receives, which refers to how many people click on and interact with the site. For there to be many clicks, the customers need to be driven towards the site. This is where search engine optimization becomes crucial, as it will enhance the traffic to the website.

Search engine optimization is often referred to as a collection of strategies whose sole purpose is to increase the amount of visitors going to a website. When a person is looking for information online, they are likely to start by visiting a search engine, and then typing what they are looking for. Often, this results in millions of search results to look through.

Proper SEO management and utilization will help to ensure that when a search is carried out on a search engine, the first results will drive the person to the website of the small business. It all lies in the phrasing and words that are used to ensure that a website becomes, and remains, significant among the sea of millions of sites.

When creating a website, small businesses can increase the traffic, as well as ensure that they are amongst the first results during a search, by ensuring that they have elements that are search engine friendly on their websites. These elements will usually take the form of keywords, which will drive people to the site and hopefully result in sales. The reason this is so important is it offers small businesses an opportunity to stand out from all other websites that are available online. However, SEO is not just about building search engine-friendly websites. It is about making a website better for people too. Even though search engine optimization almost guarantees a significant amount of customers, it has some attributes that are essential to success. The first step is to understand where the small businesses website will show up when performing a search. Will it be on the first page, or perhaps on the third or fourth page of the results? Using the right keywords will help work towards listing a website amongst the first search results.

It should be noted that quite often the ranking of search results change on a frequent basis. Therefore, it is vital for a small business to apply the right SEO strategy and to choose the right keywords for reference to their business.

It should also be noted that SEO is a long-term approach to digital marketing for small business, and should not be viewed as a quick fix to driving traffic towards a website. Building a website in a way that will be effective for driving up sales is a labor of love, one which cannot be rushed if the expected result is to be worthwhile. Moreover, search engines occasionally roll out "major" algorithmic updates (such as Google Panda and Google Penguin) that affect search results in significant ways.

Therefore, SEO should not be used as a solitary approach to digital marketing. It is a simple tool or process that helps make digital marketing more effective. With the right investment of time and resources, small businesses can look forward to long-term success as a result of properly utilizing search engine optimization.

## Quick Tips on SEO

SEO has undergone a series of evolutions over the years. To small business owners unfamiliar with the technical side of web development, the idea of Google's algorithm often seems extraordinarily complex. True enough, the algorithm itself is extraordinarily complex, but that does not mean they need an extraordinarily complex strategy to be successful with it.

Here are some basic SEO configurations that are very easy to implement and sometimes this is all that is needed to enhance exposure on major search engines.

### 1. Optimize titles, URL and descriptions

This is probably one of the oldest tips in the SEO industry, but it is still the most important. Examine the website and see if improvements can be made to the titles and descriptions, this is the first priority and a great first step for getting better rankings.

## 2. Provide useful and fresh content

One of the key reasons for a website to have a blog is to provide content to build an audience. This keeps the existing readers happy and helps a business gain new leads or customers. The website is a living, breathing entity on the internet. Every update made to the "live" website plays a crucial role in its interaction with visitors, customers, and search engines. In simple terms, if a small business updates their website frequently with high-quality content, search engines will love them for it. And with more content, it also means that there are more keywords for search engine indexing and ranking, giving small businesses more chance to attract visitors to their websites.

## 3. Improve the website's loading time

Page Speed can be described in either "loading time" (the time it takes to fully display the content on a particular page) or "time to first byte" (time taken for the browser to receive the first byte of data from the server). Either way, a faster page speed is always better. Google has indicated that page speed is one of the factors used by its algorithm to rank pages. In a way, it is also a crucial factor that affects the user experience. With good user experience, a website can retain its visitors longer. When a website loads quickly, visitors are likely to visit more than one page before they leave.

## 4. Register the website with Google and Bing webmaster tools

Google provides various tools for the SEO arsenal. The most widely used tool is Google Analytics, which offers an in-depth analytics suite to help its users understand and improve traffic to their website. Google's Webmaster Tools, however, give the advanced search expert another perspective on planning and evaluating his or her search efforts.

Google's Webmaster Tools are necessary tools for any strong SEO effort. In a nutshell, it helps webmasters to see their websites as how Google sees it. The toolset gives insights into what pages have been indexed on the site, what links are pointing to it, the most popular keywords, and much more. A site that is active in Webmaster Tools has a better shot at being fully indexed and ranked better in search results. The same goes for Bing Webmaster Tools.

## 5. Build links by making contents shareable

A key factor in SEO is link-building. Distributing links to fresh content on the website across multiple social networking platforms is a useful method to get traffic to the website itself. This strategy exponentially multiplies the number of places where visitors can discover the page and visit it. Therefore, it is vital to integrate social sharing tools to allow visitors to share the content or the website easily.

Rocket Into Digital

## Digital Trends

There are a significant number of digital marketing tools and trends in addition to Facebook and a website that can elevate the performance of a small business. Some of these tools are Google AdWords and Google Display Network, which shall be addressed in the next few chapters. As a small business, one must keep up-to-date with the latest technology and the emerging trends, so that the company can stay ahead of the competition. This section shall cover five of the most prominent digital trends in recent years and these trends will most probably affect how digital marketing will evolve.

## Infographics

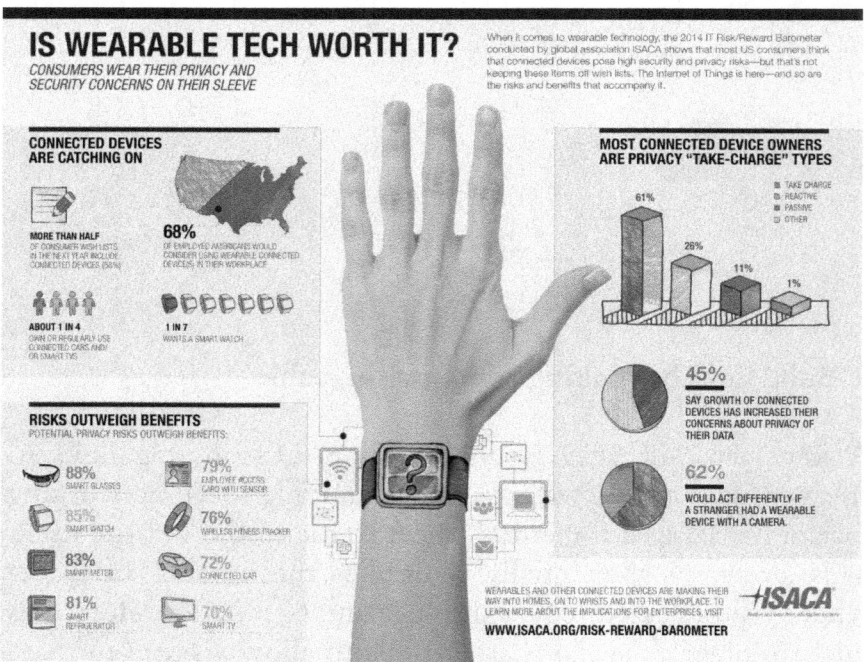

*Infographics on Wearable Tech*

There is a saying "A picture speaks a thousand words," and that is definitely the case in digital marketing. The eyes are an extension of the brain and well over half of the population are visual learners. With this in mind, publishers and businesses can benefit from changing the way they communicate their messages. There is a demand for data that is quickly transferable, coherent and visually interesting. Infographics are pictorial representations of a marketing message, and are more appealing to the average consumer than plain text. They are very versatile in regards to the information that one can include within them, and also in how one can share them. There are social networks which allow the sharing of these types of content as sponsored ads. By creating visually appealing and quality infographics, businesses can enhance the share-ability of the content, allowing more people to share and see these advertisements.

Infographics are also excellent for small businesses as they can grab the consumer's attention, and lead them to click and land on the website. They are also information in addition to being visually appealing, and with the clutter that occurs in advertising, they make it much easier to stand out. In fact, more consumers are likely to click on an advertisement that is visually appealing, than on one that has a solid block of text.

**E-commerce Facilitation**

E-commerce will rule shopping in ever-growing percentages. Research by business.com shows that 92 percent of women consumers cite online reviews as extremely/very important, and 85 percent say they always/most of the time seek them out for specific products they may want to buy. From another study done by Google (Consumer Barometer), the result shows that in many countries, the internet is an important method for purchasing products and better availability is often a reason for buying online internationally.

Thus, it is important for small businesses to realize the power of e-commerce. The result of marketing activities should ideally be a sale or the development of a customer relationship. Small businesses need to make it easier for their customers to commit to their products and make purchases. They should also ensure that their website or web portal is e-commerce enabled.

However, many small businesses do not have the technical accumen to create an e-commerce website. Thus, they can also leverage established online marketplaces such as Taobao, Amazon or eBay to get their products listed and purchased by consumers worldwide.

E-commerce allows for financial transactions to be carried out online, much in the same way as they would be at a physical store. The purpose of e-commerce facilitation is convenience, for both the customer and the small business. This is a strong factor that entices modern consumers due to their busy lifestyle. There is a growing trend of consumers who opt for online shopping rather than a physical store. E-commerce does not always mean that the end-result is a payment or has financial implications. A website can also help a small business by allowing a potential customer to make and confirm an appointment at the physical premises, making a video conference call, or downloading pertinent information. In short, it should allow result-oriented communication to take place on a digital platform.

# More than Facebook: Understanding SEO and Digital Trends

*RedMart - Singapore's reliable online supermarket*

*Taobao - One of the World's Largest Online Marketplace by Alibaba Group*

## Develop an Application

Digital marketing extends beyond the computer screen to mobile devices, so it makes sense to develop an application that can be accessed easily on both these platforms. This also depends on the type of business that one is doing, and this trend or strategy does not work with all businesses. However, it is an excellent way to engage the customer which is the goal of a small business.

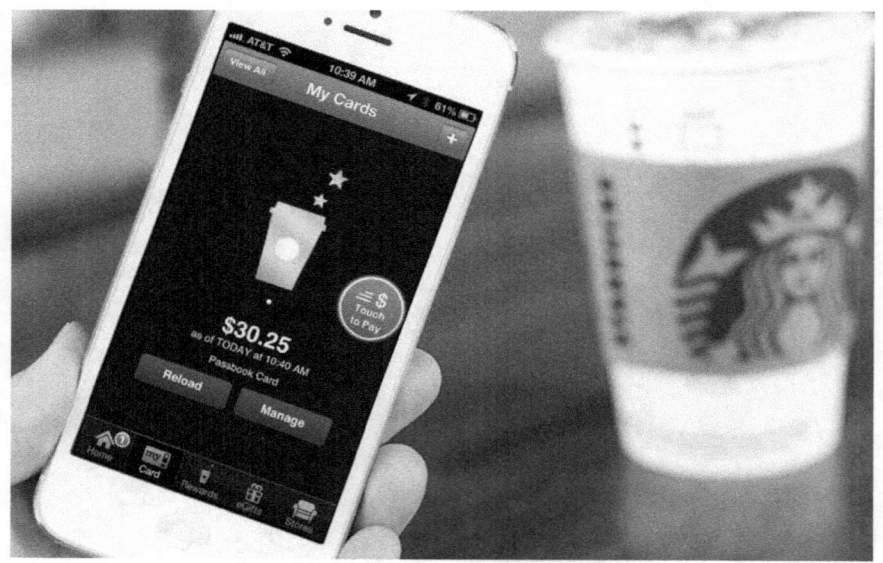

*Starbucks® app*

Applications also make it easier to send an instant message to customers, and be assured that they have received these messages. By nature of constantly using mobile devices, it is very likely that an excellent application will be the go-to reference point for any customer. If the application makes working with a small business much easier, then the customers are likely to interact with an application every time they

## More than Facebook: Understanding SEO and Digital Trends

require something from the business. For example, Starbucks has introduced the Starbucks app to their customers, giving them the quickest, easiest way to pay for their coffee. Customers can make use of the multiple features of the app including paying for their orders, earning and tracking Rewards, checking balances, adding funds to their Starbucks card, sending gift cards, and much more. This application provides convenience for their customers, and in turn, provides a positive experience with the brand.

**Wearable Technology and Internet of Things (IoT)**

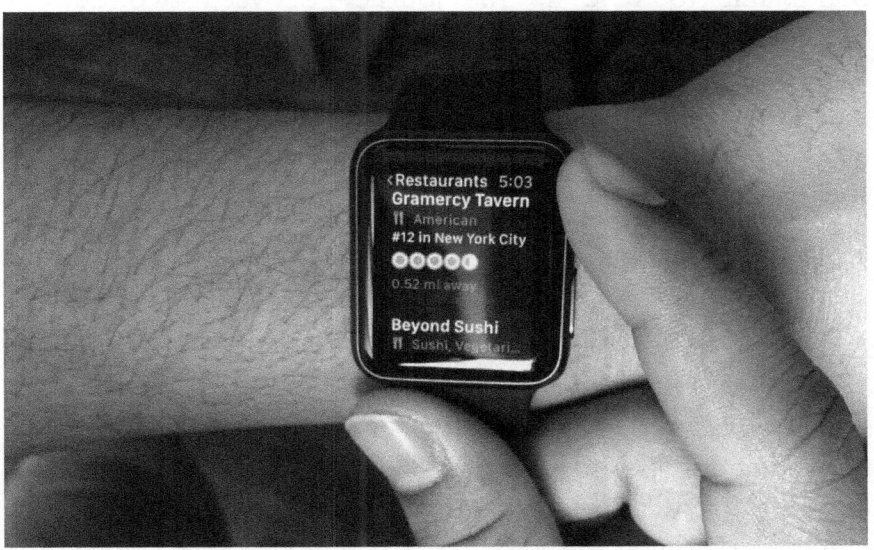

*TripAdvisor Launches Apple Watch App for Timely Travel Advice*

According to Business Insider, consumer use of wearable technology is expected to grow 35% per year between 2015 and 2019. It is amazing what these gadgets can do and how they influence the lifestyle of consumers – from telling users their heart rate, informing the doctor of their vitals to even reading the glucose levels through the use of a contact lens from Google. Wearable technology has significantly changed and integrated into the life of modern people. As more people start to use their smartwatches and other wearables, the traffic to apps will begin to increase. This could mean that traffic starts to move directly from the apps rather than search engines. People will no longer search but will go directly to their favorite app where they can consume the content of their choice.

Being able to sync up the journey between two devices (smartphones and wearables) or even moving through to tablet and desktop devices could help further improve the consumer journey, making people less likely to use search to compare other options. Wearables have changed how businesses can engage their customers.

## Analytics

As technology progresses, there is an increased emphasis on big data. One of the largest advantages of digital marketing for small business is the ability to evaluate the translation of marketing efforts into end user sales. One recent study by The Future Buzz identifies that the biggest talent and hiring gap in online marketing is in the analytics space. Very few analysts are trained in digital marketing analytics, especially when it comes to more advanced analytics.

This data is important as it can help businesses evaluate their digital marketing performance on multiple dimensions to get the big picture.

Creating and implementing an analytics program requires four basic steps:

1. Defining the key metrics and developing a plan
2. Collecting the data
3. Developing reporting features and capabilities
4. Ongoing analysis and implementation

Understanding each of these core components allows a business to make the right decision at the right time to yield the desired ROI. Successfully building a data plan is more than just identifying tools or learning how to understand charts from data. Instead, businesses should create a culture that values data and ensuring that critical business decisions are data-driven, consistently finding ways to drive data deeper into the DNA of itself.

## Quick Tips on Analytics

Here are a few metrics that one should know:

**1. Pageviews** - This measures the total number of times a website's pages are viewed. If a page is viewed more than once in a session, each view counts towards this number.

**2. Unique Pageviews** - This measures a pageview once per user session regardless of the number of times the users comes back to the page, giving a clearer picture of engagement for that page.

**3. Pages/Session** - This is the average number of pages viewed during a session.

**4. Avg. Time on Page** - This metric shows the average time users spend on a specific page.

**5. Bounce Rate** - Bounce Rate measures single-page visits, where users entered and exited a website from the same page.

**6. Audience** - This section outlines who visits the site and their demographics, along with the number of views the content receives.

**7. Acquisition** - This section reveals how users are getting to the site, whether through advertisements, organic or direct search, or referral links from other websites.

**8. Behavior** - This section can show what users are doing while they are on the website.

**9. Sessions** - Google defines a session as, "a group of interactions that take place on the website within a given time frame."

"If you do build a great experience, customers tell each other about that. Word of mouth is very powerful."

- Jeff Bezos (Founder, Amazon.com)

**Rocket Into Digital**

52

# Chapter 4

# Making the Most from Google

It can be widely argued that the most popular search engine on the internet is Google. Google is so popular that it now appears in the Merriam-Webster dictionary as a noun, and the action of using Google is a verb known as google or googling. Every small business that wants to market digitally should ensure that they take advantage of the numerous avenues and opportunities that can be explored using Google.

Whether consumers are shopping for corn flakes, concert tickets or a honeymoon in Paris, the internet has changed how they decide what to buy. In 2011, Google introduced this online decision-making moment the Zero Moment of Truth - or simply ZMOT. This theory describes a revolution in the way consumers search for information online and make decisions about brands.

Marketers have traditionally focused on three steps in the consumer-buying journey, but with the inception of the internet, a fourth step has emerged as a significant influencer on the buying journey. In the first step, also known as "stimulus," potential customers are prompted to explore a product, usually through advertisements. They then head to the store, whether physical or virtual, to buy the product. This second step is called the "first moment of truth." Finally, in the final step, the consumer experiences the product, fulfilling the "second moment of truth."

*The Traditional 3-Step Mental Model*

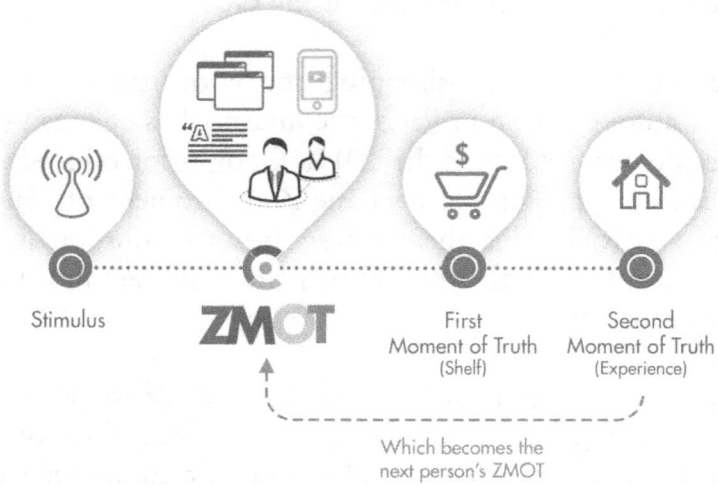

*The New Mental Model*

With easy access to a myriad of products, most consumers now conduct preliminary research prior to purchasing anything. A study funded by Google shows that the majority of consumers go online to make an informed decision when it is time to buy, whether they want a new car or just a new book. Other than to look at specific models of the product they are interested in, people conduct a more general search. Therefore, a fourth step has come out of the woodwork: the "zero moment of truth."

Marketing with the ZMOT in mind can help marketers, both traditional and digital, reach out to their target consumers more effectively, which can result in increased sales. Google Adwords and Google Display Network are also tools that Google has introduced to help businesses 'touch' their target customers at the ZMOT stage.

**Google AdWords**

Google AdWords refer to advertisements that can be found through Google searches, and these ads are known for having a large impact. Google AdWords is one of the primary digital marketing tools that is used by Google. It can significantly increase digital marketing effectiveness. It generally operates on a pay per click principle, where marketers only make payments for an advertisement once a client has interacted with it through clicking.

This bidding strategy is excellent for a small business that is looking for an efficient option when advertising. Digitally, like on traditional platforms, potential customers may see an advertisement, but may not react ideally because of it. By using the pay per click strategy, it is easier to make a more accurate estimation on customers who are interested in using the product or service. At the same time, it allows business to make use of their marketing budget effectively.

Small businesses can use Google AdWords to increase their leads and build up their customer base. With the right campaign, it becomes possible to increase quality website traffic and convert this traffic into a potential lead or sale. However, for this to occur, Google AdWords must be used correctly. It is imperative that the advert uses the right search term variables, and the marketer should have considered the appropriate return on investment factors.

When many small businesses consider digital marketing using Google AdWords, what may come to mind is the expense. After all, large companies are using the same tool and have budgets large enough to take over most of the advertising space on the search engine. Luckily, there is no need to spend an enormous amount of money on Google AdWords to build a business. What one needs to do is make sure that the right people are clicking on the messages. At the same time, AdRank in AdWords has historically been calculated based on the Max CPC (cost per click) and Quality Score, meaning small businesses can still compete fairly with bigger corporations with a huge budget, if they apply the correct strategies.

For this to happen, a small business marketer must ensure that the marketing message has an explicit goal before getting started. Some goals that are often considered include growing the sales of the business, increasing awareness, and driving traffic to the website. AdWords is best used for increasing the sales of a business, as this goal is the easiest one to measure. When creating the advert, there should be some call-to-action, such as requiring the client to make a call or finalize a purchase.

## Making the Most from Google

By setting a clear and measurable goal, businesses can determine the success of their AdWords campaign.

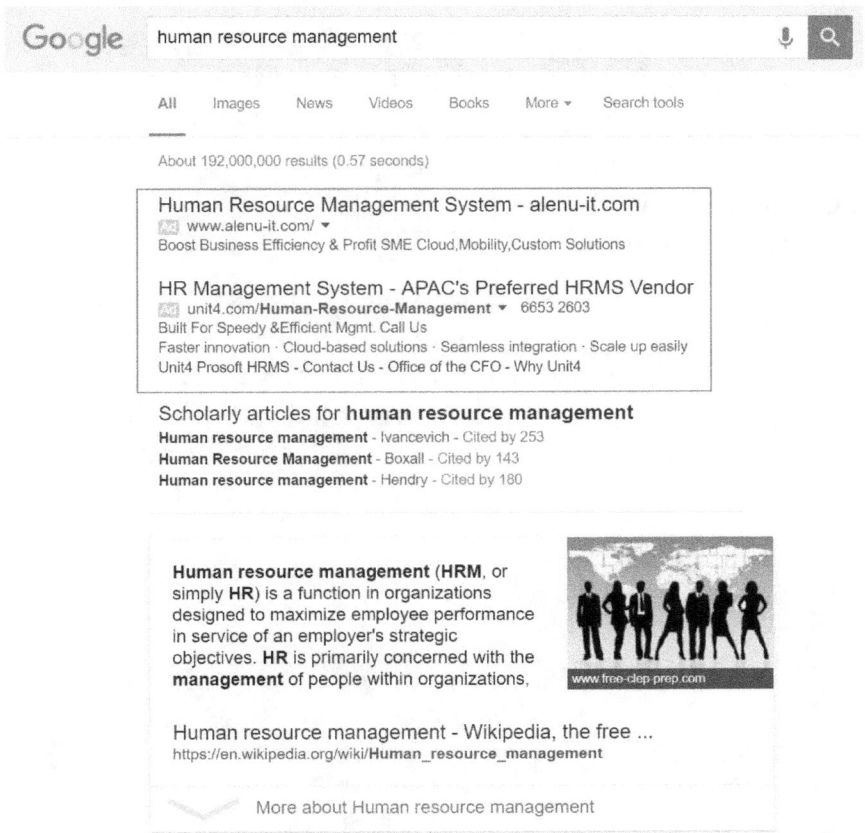

*Google AdWords on Search Result*

The words that are used in the AdWords campaign should have the target market in mind. Some marketers use words that are not entirely truthful in their ads to increase web traffic. This should be avoided entirely, as this could be the one way to kill a campaign by misleading the audience.

Rocket Into Digital

## Quick Tips on Google AdWords

**AD RANK = CPC BID × QUALITY SCORE**

The best combined **CPC Bid X Quality Score** gets the best position:

 This is the maximum bid one specify for his/her keyword.

 This is a metric to determine how relevant and useful the ad is to the user. The higher the quality score, the better.

| | Max Bid | | Quality Score | Ad Rank | |
|---|---|---|---|---|---|
| Advertiser I | $2.00 | | 10 ★★★★★★★★★★ | 20 | 🥇 |
| Advertiser II | $4.00 | | 4 ★★☆☆☆★★☆☆☆ | 16 | |
| Advertiser III | $6.00 | | 2 ★★☆☆☆☆☆☆☆☆ | 12 | |
| Advertiser IV | $8.00 | | 1 ★☆☆☆☆☆☆☆☆☆ | 8 | |

Notice how with a lower CPC Bid, Advertiser I still can outbid Advertiser IV with a higher max CPC.

# Making the Most from Google

Some of the factors that affect the Quality Score:

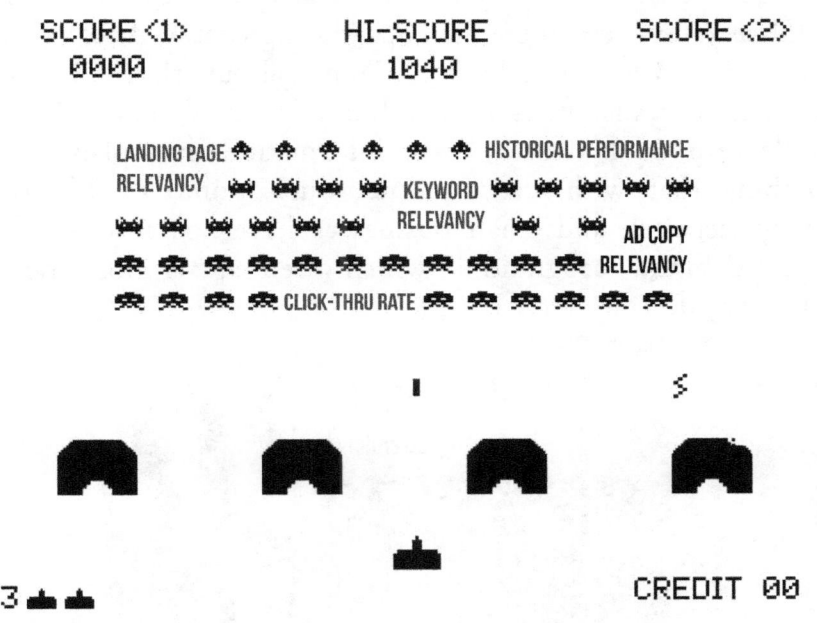

1. Landing Page Relevancy
2. Keyword Relevancy
3. Ad Copy Relevancy
4. Click-Through Rate
5. Historical Performance

In a nutshell, higher quality ads typically lead to lower costs and better ad positions. The AdWords system works best for everybody – advertisers, customers, publishers, and Google – when the ads are relevant, closely matching what customers are looking for. Relevant ads tend to earn more clicks, appear in a higher position, and bring business the most success.

Rocket Into Digital

## Google Display Network (GDN)

The use of custom imagery in display ads can provide a lift in brand searches, search engine click-through rates, direct visits and online/offline purchasing. Think about this: 90% of information transmitted to the brain is visual and 40% of people respond better to visual information than plain text. Combine that with the multiple touch points within the display network and small businesses have got a recipe for increased brand recognition - which often equals more traffic and more sales.

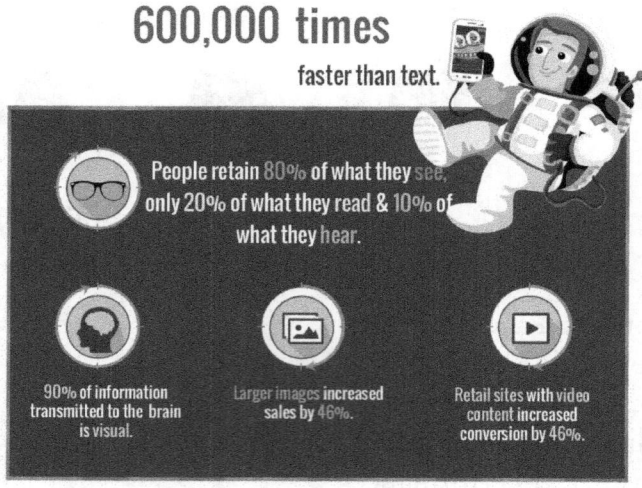

*The Power of Visuals*

The Google Display Network is used by thousands of marketers to reach consumers on hundreds of thousands of websites and apps across all publisher categories, from large, well-known sites to niche sites and audiences. In simple terms, the GDN will place display ads against related content and audiences across thousands of sites.

## Making the Most from Google

GDN is made up of a collection of websites that include some Google sites such as the Blogger, YouTube, Gmail and Finance, as well as some mobile sites and apps. Marketers can also choose which of the available publisher sites or pages they would like their advertisement to appear on, as well as the most appealing format. When showing ads on the display network, small businesses can reach a broad range of customers with multiple targeting options, and engage users with appealing ad formats.

According to statistics, the display network reaches 90% of internet users globally, and includes more than 2 million publisher sites like nytimes.com and weather.com (Source: Comscore 2013). With flexible pricing models like Cost Per Thousand Impressions (CPM), Cost Per Click (CPC) and Cost Per Aquisition (CPA), the Google Display Network is a useful tool for small business to reach out to their targeted audience if they want to use interactive ad formats at the ZMOT stage. It can help drive results every day for thousands of small businesses around the world.

Text Ads on websites    Image Ads on websites    Video Ads on websites    Ads on Mobile Websites

*Different Ad Formats for Google Display Network*

## Remarketing

Remarketing is a clever way to connect with visitors to a website who may not have made an ideal call-to-action, which may include an immediate purchase or enquiry. It allows businesses to position targeted ads in front of a defined audience that had previously visited their website - as they browse elsewhere around the internet.

The remarketing ads can be delivered in either or both text and image display formats. The ads are managed in Google AdWords and are shown on web pages visited by the targeted audience that accepts Google advertising placements.

Google remarketing is an ideal tactic particularly when the sales process is long and considered competitive. Executed in the right way it can be a powerful tool to improve sales conversions and to raise the brand profile of small businesses.

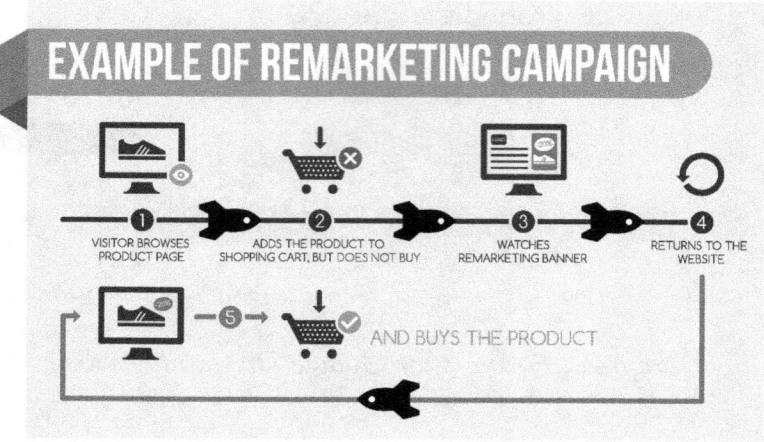

*How Remarketing Works*

"You can't wait for customers to come to you. You have to figure out where they are, go there and drag them back to your store."

- Paul Graham (Y COMBINATOR)

**Rocket Into Digital**

# Chapter 5

## Build the Brand by Maximizing Social Media Presence

In the previous chapters, there was mention of Facebook and the marketing benefits of this platform. Facebook falls within a larger scope of networking sites that are identified as Social Media sites. Within social media, there are social networking sites, which are highly popular digital meeting places for people all over the world.

On social networking sites, people are willing to share information, have discussions, exchange pictures, videos – basically interact as they would in a face to face situation, but, in this case, they do it remotely. When there is a platform for people to have this kind of interaction, marketers can also experience finding a ready market to share their message.

When one intends to build their market using social media, it is vital to understand the different social media platforms, learn about their best practices, identify their user demographics, and learn how to advertise effectively on them. This is because there are so many different types of platforms available, and the effects that these advertisements have on the different communities are likely to vary, which will also influence the development of the business. This section shall review the most popular social networking sites, and how small businesses can leverage them for financial success.

**Facebook**

This is probably the most popular social network for small businesses to advertise on, and that is due to the massive reach of a potential 1.59 billion monthly active users worldwide. Facebook marketing is popular because it allows for interaction with customers and targeted marketing. There are a good number of tools available on the site, and for that reason, marketing on Facebook requires a well thought-out strategy.

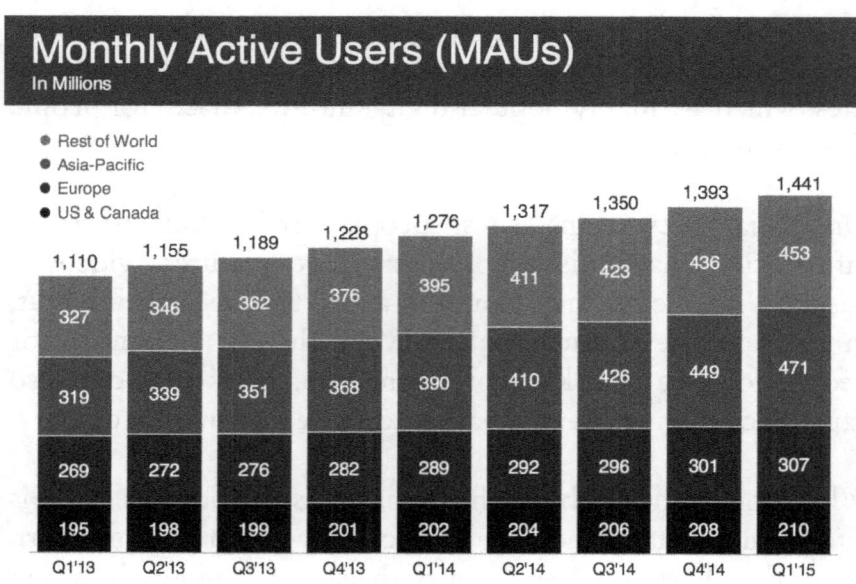

*Source: www.techinasia.com*

To get the most out of Facebook for a small business brand, the first thing that should be done is the creation of a page for the business. This page is an information and interaction platform, where a customer can find out about the business, its products and services, its web address and other contact information. It is on this page that the company will put out posts and status updates giving up-to-date information on the product or service on offer, and where customers can experience direct interaction.

This page should also be used to create a social media community, a pool of customers that are always available to receive marketing communication from the business. This pool is created when people visit the page and like it. By doing so, they agree to receive the posts from this page on their timelines so that they can read up on the latest news from the business.

Building a brand requires the business to remain constantly in the minds of the consumers, and this is an excellent way to do so. The good thing about Facebook marketing is that, for the most part, it is non-intrusive, and the customer can read through status updates while they go about their usual social networking interactions. There are also advertisements that appear on the right-hand side of the screen on Facebook, but these do not interfere in any way with the activities that a customer might be carrying out while they are on the social networking site.

For brand building, this social media platform pulls people to action through a message or a story. Traditional marketing takes an approach that is more push oriented, bombarding people with persuasive information to get them to make a purchase. However, most content creators nowadays are embarking on a thought-leadership marketing strategy whereby they position their company as a leader in its field through best-in-class content, providing appealing and high-quality content on social media.

Facebook also has tools that facilitate campaigns at flexible costs and multiple bidding options. For a small business, this is great because it ensures that the only advertising that is paid for is that which results in an interaction with the targeted audience as determined by the campaign strategist. If a potential customer views an advert but does not take any action, then they do not have to pay for that view.

**Pros:**
- With over 1 billion users, small businesses are guaranteed to find a large number of people within their targeted demographics.
- This platform lends itself well to engagement as fans who like a page or users that have not liked a page can both like, comment on, and share posts.
- Businesses can promote their posts or pages to reach a wider audience and introduce the business to potential new followers or customers.
- The use of hashtags makes it easy for businesses to spread their messages to an audience that is searching within Facebook for what they have to offer.

**Cons:**
- Any negative feedback will be visible.
- With constant updates on the Facebook walls, posts may get lost in the mix.
- Investing in paid advertising is the best option if a small business is just starting out.

## Quick Tips on Facebook

It is no secret that paid advertising is becoming an essential part of social media campaigns. If one has dabbled in paid advertising, there is no doubt that composing the perfect Facebook advert takes time and practice.

### 1. Know the audience

The priority is the creation of marketing personas to target the needs of the audience. Relevance is the key to success for marketing campaigns, and the audience businesses choose will affect how much they pay and how well the campaign performs.

There are a ton of targeting options available: from demographics (such as age and gender) to behaviors (people who connect to Facebook through mobile devices) and then, of course, targeting based on interests.

### 2. Be consistent

The tone, branding, and images need to match the message on the landing page. If one is promoting watches and the Facebook advert says there is a 30% off watches on sale, then that will be what people are expecting from the landing page. All too often great adverts are let down by not choosing the most relevant images and landing page on the website.

### 3. Use a professional image

Research done by HubSpot found that content with relevant

images can receive up to 94% more views than content without. When it comes to that perfect image, a professional stock image can go a long way. Not only will good quality images help an advert look more professional, but they can also contribute to improving the advert's Relevance Score.

## 4. Use a clear call to action

No good advert is complete without a clear call to action, pointing the audience in the right direction. Having a well-crafted advert with a strong call to action will not only help to increase conversions of the campaign, but it will make an advert stand out from the rest and get an improved click-through rate. Studies have proven that the inclusion of a call to action button can improve click-through rates by up to 3 times the average.

## 5. Schedule advert

To get maximum impact for a campaign, one should be scheduling adverts at times when it appeals to the targeted audience. For instance, if one is looking to get more customers into a restaurant, ads should be planned to appear at critical times such as lunchtime, mid-afternoon and early evening when Facebook activity is high. These times will also be the period when consumers are making their meal decisions, reaching them at the perfect micro-moments.

## 6. Learn from insights

As with any form of digital marketing, data is a friend. Learning from insights from past campaigns will help small businesses to see what worked for them - and what did not.

## Build the Brand by Maximizing Social Media Presence

From working out which options and setups respond the best to their adverts, Insights can be a powerful tool that can help businesses get the most from their marketing budget.

## Twitter

This is an excellent social media platform that allows a registered account holder to send messages that are short when only 140 characters are allowed per message. It is often referred to as the phone of social networks, as it allows for quick conversations between parties, just as can be expected with a brief phone call. This network was popularized by celebrities who were looking for an outlet where they could speak directly to their fans. Small businesses can use this as a platform to do the very same thing – interact directly with their customers.

This entails more than sending out a few tweets (messages on Twitter) on a daily basis. To build a brand, the focus shifts from simply sending a message, to also ensuring there is a sustained social media presence as well as an influence.

This all begins with what is called the Twitter handle. This is different from the name of the small business, which should remain professional. The Twitter handle allows for some creativity, which is excellent when trying to create an association in the mind of the consumer. When customers interact with companies on Twitter, they will refer to the company using the Twitter handle.

Small businesses also need to ensure that they fit into a Twitter niche. To do so, the small business would need to follow other businesses in the same field so they can have a look at their

## Rocket Into Digital

updated messages. This type of connection also makes it easier for the customers to identify with the business.

Building a brand also requires some repetition. Therefore, to ensure the business reach their market, they should send the same tweet out several times a day. This is important to remember, particularly for small businesses. The reason being, Twitter will completely renew the dashboard every 15 minutes.

There is also a need to build up the number of followers that businesses have so that they can reach a significant number of people with their marketing messages. The best way to do this is to try live tweeting, which entails creating a marketing campaign for a limited period of time. During this campaign, the small business marketer can have a two-way conversation with potential clientele by tweeting on the same subjects, referring to them personally, and answering all enquiries in real time.

*Hashtags on Twitter*

Twitter also uses hashtags in messaging. A hashtag creates a trend, which is what happens when many people are talking about the same issue. With a creative digital marketing campaign, a small business can work towards the point of trending, as this will attract a whole host of new customers. Trending means that their customers will be referring to their activities using the hashtag that can be seen all around the world, rather than just the Twitter handle.

**Pros:**
- The use of hashtags makes it easy for business to spread their messages to an audience that is searching within Twitter for what they have to offer.
- Followers can easily favorite posts and retweet messages to their followers and vice versa, which leads to high levels of engagement.

**Cons:**
- If followers follow a lot of other accounts, tweets could easily be pushed to the bottom of their feed and get lost.
- The 140 characters limit will constrain the amount of information that can be included in a tweet.
- Negative tweets can spread like wildfire.

## Instagram and Pinterest

There is a term in social media marketing known as 'going viral', and this is what these social networking sites facilitate. In traditional marketing, creating a buzz and getting people to talk about a product and interact with it are the main ways that a company can create a presence and build on its customer base. Digital marketing follows the same concept when it creates a campaign that goes viral.

When something goes viral on the internet, it means that everyone shares the message, talks about it, wants to see it, and is willing to interact with the message by leaving comments, reviews or taking action. If a small business manages to create a campaign that can go viral, they are assured that they will engage new customers and retain older ones.

A viral campaign is like the word of mouth of digital marketing. In marketing, this is the most powerful tool for a business that is looking to grow. Customers tend to believe each other much more than they do marketing messages that are sent out from the business. If the messages they are sharing amongst each other are positive, then more people are encouraged to interact with the business on a digital platform. If these messages are negative, and are not addressed by the business, then customers are likely to lose faith and choose not to interact with the small business.

Instagram and Pinterest are primarily visual sites where one can post pictures and short videos. They are platforms for a small business to offer a visual story about what the business stands for, and how they can be of help to customers. As part of their visual storyboard, the business can drive people to a website where they can get more information and source for products or services. As mentioned in earlier chapters, our brains love visual content, therefore, visual sites like these are highly liked by people. In some cases, visual campaigns can be highly viral.

When using this platform to build a brand, a small business is sending out a clear message that they are current, interested in customer interaction, and offer something that their clients will love and connect with.

## Pros:

- The use of hashtags makes it easy for business to spread their messages to an audience that is searching within Instagram for what they have to offer.
- If a business has a wide variety of products to showcase, this photo-sharing application is perfect for showing them off.
- If a business has visual appealing products and photos, this application is the platform to capture their targeted audience.

## Cons:

- While businesses are able to post links in the profile description, they are not able to do so in individual post descriptions.
- Primarily, one can only post through a mobile device, not through a laptop or a desktop.
- There is a need for visually appealing content to succeed in this platform.

## LinkedIn

LinkedIn is a social network for professionals and businesses, and everything on this network retains this focus. Leading thinkers from all over the world in a variety of industries use LinkedIn as a platform to give advice on business, as well as sharing their secrets to success.

A small business that uses this social networking platform to build their brand sends a clear message that they are serious about themselves and their customers. To maximize a brand on this platform, there are several steps that the small business should take.

To start, they should create a Company Page that will be their online identity on LinkedIn. LinkedIn pages also allow for Showcase Pages (Products & Services tab was removed April 14th, 2014) for product and service content. Plus, members can easily find the Showcase Page through search and by visiting the Company Page. This makes it easier for customers to identify products that are on offer, and a visual representation is often a real catalyst leading up to a sale.

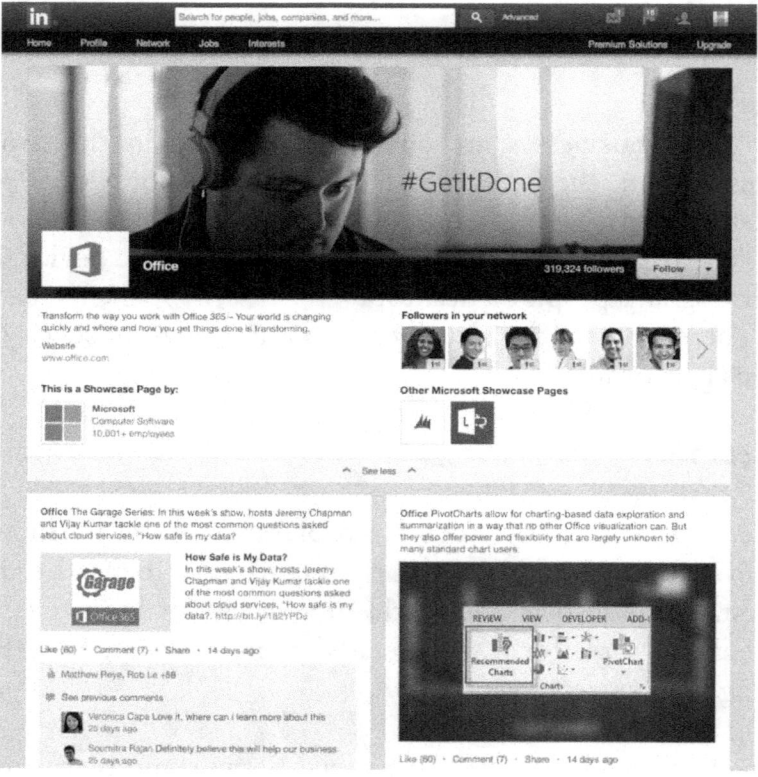

*A LinkedIn Showcase Page*

A small business can also post regular updates giving information about the brand, or even short stories that will encourage people to try the brand. This encourages consumers to learn more about the brand, and to interact with the brand – creating a platform for two-way communication. Consistent and constant status updates reminds a customer about the small businesses' existence, and if these status updates are informative and interesting, they can result in a substantial following.

LinkedIn allows for targeting according to industry. Part of building a brand is having an excellent support system to ensure that the brand can meet the customers' expectations. LinkedIn helps businesses market to each other, and in that way, create a strong support network for their operations.

**Pros:**
- LinkedIn is highly professional in nature, so by using it correctly small businesses can establish themselves as a trustworthy company who is an expert in their field or industry.
- Users on LinkedIn naturally segment themselves by industry, so once a business made an account and have established themselves, they will fall into their niche with others who will appreciate their content.

**Cons:**
- Those who spend their time on LinkedIn are generally business professionals. If the targeted audience does not match that description (stay-at-home moms, teenage boys, etc.) this platform may not be suitable for the business.
- Advertising on LinkedIn is more expensive than other social media platforms.

## Social Media Marketing Tips for Brand Building

When building a brand on social media platforms, it is important to be consistent. All online channels that the small business may have should contain similar messaging. Therefore, if there are people logging onto the website, they should see the same message as they would find in an email. This reveals that the business is clear about what it is looking to accomplish, and how they plan to do so with the customers.

Today, social networks are interconnected, making digital marketing less complicated - or so it would seem. What a small business marketer should remember when building a brand is that every social network services a different purpose, and, the messages that are posted on each network should serve their purpose. Therefore, it is not advisable to connect all social networking platforms so that they all have the same message. Social networks for individuals and pages have a facility where marketers can post a message on one, and it will automatically appear on another social networking site in exactly the same way. This type of messaging should be discouraged. The message should be skewed to fit with the objective of the social networking page, and, at the same time, adhere to the best practices of each platform.

Measuring the effects of social media marketing can be done using a social return on investment evaluation. It is one thing to have thousands of followers on social networking sites, but how can one tell that these followers are translating into sales for the business?

The best way is to evaluate the way that they are interacting with the social networking page. What is the percentage of comments that are being left on posts, in relation to the number of followers that a business has? How many people will like a post that a business places online? This will tell businesses conclusively how many people are engaging with their brand.

The next thing is to look at how many positive or negative comments businesses receive on their social networking pages, as this gives information on the customer's sentiments. Negative comments should be addressed immediately to return the customer back to a satisfied state. From the customer responses, does there appear to be an emotional connection with the brand? This is what every small business should aim to achieve. Most importantly, what is the effect on the company's bottom line? That is, after all, why small businesses have ventured into digital marketing.

Marketers should remain astute to the fact that social media platforms are public forums, and therefore, as much as they allow for free speech, the information that is posted can be used against them in the court of law. Negative language, abusive suppositions and stereotypical comments do not belong on the social networking pages of any business, big or small.

**Rocket Into Digital**

"You can't just open a website and expect people to flood in. If you really want to succeed you have to create traffic."

- Joel Anderson (CEO, Walmart)

**Rocket Into Digital**

# Chapter 6

# Why Going Digital can Triple Sales Growth

Two terms that are used interchangeably, or in relation to each other, are sales and marketing. This points to the relationship that each of these terms have with each other. If one were to try to separate their association with each other, they would end up with a situation like that of the chicken and the egg. Which came first? This is a question that is almost impossible to answer as they rely so heavily on each other. In this case, we are talking about sales and marketing.

Digital marketing allows for a closer customer interaction than traditional marketing. The multiple channels that are available on digital platforms facilitate extended customer reach as well. Through these channels, digital marketing efforts are able to translate into sales.

On traditional marketing platforms, it is sometimes difficult to measure the effects that an advertisement has, especially the translation from advertising into sales. A small business may make an investment to market by placing a massive billboard in a location with heavy customer traffic. The result could be that everyone is aware of the business and its products and services, but they are not motivated to make a purchase. The challenge that small businesses then face is: how do they get their customers to take action and make a purchase?

Digital platforms have various strategies that can be employed to ensure that every effort they make translates into sales or equally desirable activities. The first is to have fresh and interactive content to captivate consumers. Billboards and print media tend to be static. The message remains the same for several weeks or months, and this makes it easier for the customer to block the message out. Having fresh content allows small businesses to benefit from rapidly changing consumer tastes and even trends, and to stay ahead of the competition. When the content is interesting and of high quality, customers are encouraged to remain on a website or landing page, and find out more about a product, the result being that they are more likely to make a purchase or convert.

Another reason that digital marketing is excellent for small businesses is because online data or analytics can be the fuel that drives success. Technology is now catching up to the holy grail of marketing: the ability to monitor, track, and manage the effectiveness of marketing investments. Marketers must collect, understand and integrate this useful information into their marketing strategy to optimize their marketing efforts. With such data, companies can then make data-driven decisions and right investments at the right time to yield an ROI.

## Multi-channel Digital Platforms

Digital platforms are numerous, allowing customers to be reached with more than their computers or laptops. Mobile devices have expanded the reach of most companies as well as increased the level of interaction. By opting for a multi-channel approach across numerous digital platforms, the customer is reminded more often of the product or service and is, therefore, more likely to make a purchase.

Having sites that can access different platforms is changing companies and affecting their growth. It now makes more economic senses to have a marketing strategy that is more digitalized than those that use traditional mediums. The return on investment is much higher. Mobile marketing is a real driving force behind tripling sales growth, as customers will now spend hours every day on their mobile devices while they are going about their day-to-day activities. Therefore, websites now have the option of being mobile optimized, allowing for better viewing and interaction with the customer. Taking this a step further, there are now mobile applications being developed to enhance a customer's social interaction with a site, product or service.

*People look at their mobile phones while waiting for a train at a subway station in Tokyo (Source: Reuters)*

There is no doubt that consumers today have much more control over the buying process than marketers do. Thanks to the proliferation of available channels, customers have more choices than ever when it comes to how they want to get information.

Therefore, multi-channel marketing is important for small businesses simply because they must be where the customers are. In most cases, the customers are everywhere. Thus, other than just investing in traditional marketing, businesses must look into digital marketing to reach out to their customers at the micro-moments. Micro-moments are periods when consumers act on a need, e.g. to do, learn, discover, watch or buy something. They are intent-rich moments where decisions are being made and preferences are being shaped. Another strength of multi-channel marketing is that multichannel customers have a tendency to spend three to four times more than single-channel customers do.

## Retargeting (Remarketing Revisited)

Going digital also makes it possible to experience the benefits of retargeting. This is one of the latest marketing techniques on digital platforms, and it almost guarantees an increase in sales, due to getting the right information to the right customers. It works by keeping track of customers using their cookies.

When a customer is online, they leave a trail of what pages they have accessed and the particular information that they were looking for on those sites. With so many websites to browse through and choose from, what often happens is that customers will look through one site, and continue browsing through a few more before making a purchase decision. If there is too much information available, a customer can end up overwhelmed. As a result, no sales are finalized at all. At this juncture, the customer may log off the computer or device.

Retargeting gives a reminder to the customer, redirecting them back to a site that they may have browsed through, but failed to make a purchase. It works by ensuring that ads are strategically placed on individual websites display information based on the cookies that a customer has created. Therefore, the customer can take a second look at a product or service, and a reminder from a particular site may call the customer to action.

Dynamic remarketing takes this to the next level by including the products or services that people viewed on the website within the ads. While dynamic remarketing takes additional steps such as adding custom parameters to the website's tag and creating a feed, it can deliver customized, higher-performance ads, which can result in increased sales. This is a technique that small businesses should take advantage of if they are looking to significantly increase their sales and growth. Repeat reminders are more likely to result in higher sales for the small business. This method also helps to elevate the profile of the brand.

## Convenience

Consumers today have less and less time for activities outside of work and family. In order to survive, and to prosper financially, people are spending more time at the workplace, leaving less time for them to visit small businesses for the purchase of products or services. This does not mean that they are no longer buying required commodities. Instead, it points to different channels for purchasing that are more convenient and flexible, fitting into their busy schedules. In some cases, even if they do purchase from a physical store, the internet is still an important resource for people looking to research their product prior to purchase.

For this reason, many businesses are now offering their services on online platforms. They are able to serve the customer by delivering the products once an order has been made. Consider the world's leading online stores, one of which is Amazon. They are able to sell products effectively to their clients on a digital platform, and these products are delivered to the customers. This cuts out the need for the customer to visit a physical store when making a purchase.

Regular businesses, like supermarkets, are also following this trend of availing their products for sale online in an attempt to increase their sales growth, and it is working. In fact, what seems to be happening now is a trend, where large stores are becoming smaller, but their digital outreach is becoming more aggressive. Marketing digitally reduces operational costs significantly, but the yield, on the other hand, increases substantially. For many such businesses, they can also integrate analytics and digital marketing with their online store to reach out to their targeted audience more effectively, and thus increase their sales.

## Case Study: The Changing Music Industry

An excellent example of how going digital can triple sales growth can be seen in the music industry. Traditionally, artists sell their works via tapes, which then graduated to CD's (compact discs). The advent of the internet led to downloading music and decreased revenue from CD sales. At that point, it

## Why Going Digital can Triple Sales Growth

was time to make a technological change. In order to remain relevant, and to make sure that their music can be heard and enjoyed by the masses, artists ended up selling their singles and albums on digital platforms.

Talk about the transformation of an industry! Today, no artist would consider releasing an album without access to a digital platform. Digital platforms such as YouTube, Spotify, iTunes, and SoundCloud are part of this phenomenon. These platforms make it easier for artists to market and sell their music at seemingly nominal prices. However, when the volume of possible sales is evaluated, it is clear that a digital platform can lead to significant commercial success, a much higher success than an artist would have benefited from by selling their music in physical form.

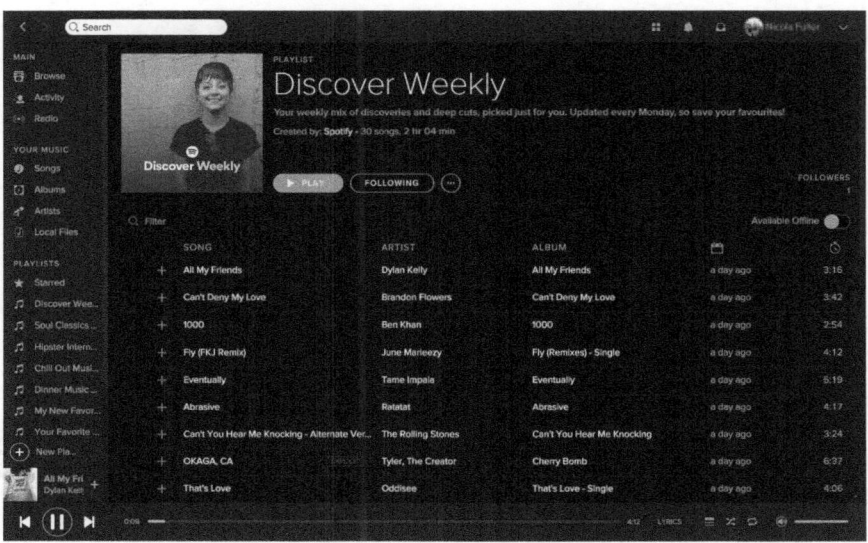

*Discover New Music on Spotify*

### Rocket Into Digital

In many cases, little-known artists have become an overnight phenomenon due to going viral, when people share them among their social networks, contributing to fame and success. Such platforms also allow artists to build the online communities as fans, followers or subscribers that are measurable, readily available for their online campaigns and contents. Nowadays, many influential artists use the social media to build their fan bases and to communicate directly to their fans. These platforms also provide a venue for them to update their latest developments and announce news of their latest album release dates.

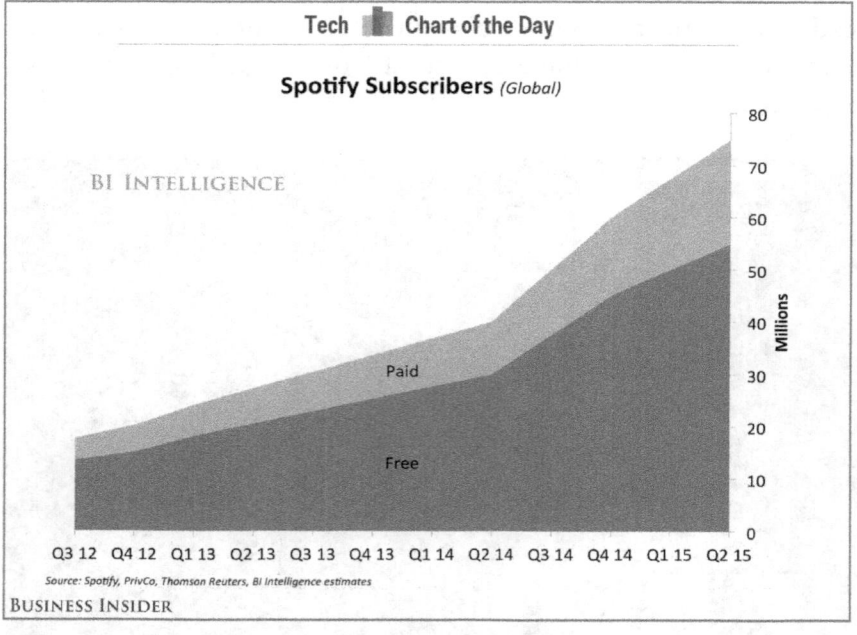

*Growth of Spotify according to Business Insider*

Artists are also able to increase their sales by offering subscriptions via streaming services online. Streaming is becoming more popular as a means to access music online, so much so that it is marginally more popular than downloading music. Digital marketing has resulted in a change in the way music is packaged for the consumers, but not in the music itself. It changes the lifestyle of the people and how music is marketed to them. New albums or singles are no longer marketed on TV as they were in the past. The rules of the game have changed significantly with the advancement of technology.

## Case Study: Cross-Channel Marketing Drives Digital Sales

For more than six decades, Land Rover has been building durable luxury SUVs. In 2013, the business was looking for new ways to create awareness for its Range Rover model and to reach out to more consumers. Realizing that the majority of today's auto shoppers begin their car purchasing journey online, Land Rover wanted to reach these buyers through all their devices at every moment in the purchasing funnel. As a result, the company partnered with Google on a cross-channel strategy that would engage shoppers at every touchpoint.

The strategy was to run cross-channel Range Rover campaigns across search, display, social media and YouTube. By using Google Display Network and YouTube, Land Rover was able to create lasting brand connections with their target consumers. On YouTube, a homepage takeover was carried out with an expandable Range Rover masthead ad that played a video when clicked by viewers. Over the span of the campaign, the ad received tens of millions of impressions across all devices and had an interaction rate of 12%. To further extend the impact of the Google Display Network, Land Rover used a new Engagement Ad format which helped the Range Rover story reach millions of users with a sizable engagement rate of

## Rocket Into Digital

3.85%.

Land Rover also used Google's remarketing feature to continue its advertising with potential buyers who had either visited LandRover.com or watched one of the unique Engagement Ads the company ran on AdWords.

Through digital marketing solutions and strategies, Land Rover has increased the digital share of its marketing budget from 15% to 37% since 2011, which resulted in the rise of sales by double digits each year. Today, an impressive 15% of Land Rover's sales come from digital, and cross-channel marketing is the key contributing factor for this growth.

*An Example of a YouTube Masthead*

## What Is In It For Small Businesses?

It points out that products and services can stay the same, but in order to triple sales growth on digital platforms, a small business needs to keep up with the ever-changing consumer trends and meet them head on. By providing what the customer wants, in the way that they want it, making enormous sales becomes possible. In many instances, businesses need to chart a plan of the best way forward in order to establish a channel that can be beneficial to them. Understanding and embracing digital marketing is also a proven way to help grow a business.

Digital growth is the future for small businesses, as the cost of brick and mortar outlets becomes unsustainable. Changing consumer behavior signals the need to change the way businesses work to ensure profitability. What is happening now is that, with emerging technologies, digital marketing and new digital platforms, consumers can engage in e-commerce activities anywhere and anytime. This means that purchases do not only occur in a physical store, but they can also happen at home, in the office, or even on public transport. All small businesses need to evolve in order to survive and excel in this new era, and therefore, ensure increased sales growth.

**Rocket Into Digital**

"Smartphones are reinventing the connection between companies and their customers."

- Rich Miner (Partner, Google Ventures)

**Rocket Into Digital**

# Chapter 7

# Rounding Up Digital Marketing Components

Now that there is a general idea of the benefits digital marketing can deliver, it is imperative to understand the different components of digital marketing that can be exploited. The components of the digital world are more than those that are mentioned in this chapter. They are ever changing and will evolve according to emerging technologies and trends. However, here are some of the essential components that will make up a digital marketing strategy, meant to capitalize on every aspect of digital marketing to build customer relationships and drive sales.

## The Website

The first and most important component of digital marketing for small businesses is the website. Every small business should ensure that they have an informative website to create a connection with their customers. Websites are low-cost tools, and, in some cases, are even available for free. Therefore, small businesses cannot excuse themselves from building and investing in a website. The website is the digital representation of the brick and mortar store and includes many other aspects as well. In the same way that a customer expects to receive excellent customer service at a physical outlet, they expect the same from a website. As customers rarely interact with a person face-to-face while they are on a website, it becomes easier for the customer to feel isolated. Thus, for websites to be effective, they should include all the information on the products and services available, contact information, a background of the business, and links to social media platforms where customers can interact with the business.

Businesses should ensure that the website is impactful and able to capture the attention of their visitors, and this requires an excellent design. That is why there is an increasing emphasis on UI/UX (user interface and user experience) and the importance of the first impressions. Good design boosts the amount of trust a visitor has in a website and therefore increases their confidence in the business. It also speaks about the brand identity of the business. Bad design, on the other hand, sends them bouncing away in search of something more reliable. In fact, the design of the website impacts every single moment a visitor spends on a page. It can make the difference between a great user experience and a lousy one, ultimately determining the conversions.

When design focuses on user interface and user experience, it delivers measurable results to the business in the form of more conversions on the sales pages, increased frequency, and number of sales, and a more profitable bottom line.

On April 2015, Google released a significant new mobile-friendly ranking algorithm that is designed to give higher priority to mobile-friendly pages in Google's search results.

## Rounding Up Digital Marketing Components

With so many websites and landing pages not optimized for mobile, it was hard not to be skeptical about the potential impact of this update. Thus, in recent years, it has also become a requirement for websites to be mobile responsive, so that they can provide a more positive user experience, and rank better on Google.

*An Example of a Mobile Friendly Website*

Many platforms offer free templates for web development, and these should be avoided by the serious digital marketer. Making an impact requires an original product, and one thing that will make a small business stand out from larger players in the market is excellent creativity.

In the same way, that social media networks should have frequent status updates, websites also need to have constant and updated news. When someone visits a website they should find new information each time, showing that the company is progressing and up-to-date with the customer's needs. This requires proper website development, which includes the maintenance of the website and some technical knowledge to "upgrade" the website with the latest trends and technologies. Small business owners often try to operate their websites on their own, but for a positive effect, they should occasionally consider outsourcing a digital marketing specialist or a good developer to manage their website professionally. If the budget is available, having a member of staff that is dedicated to maintaining a website and its social media profiles could be enormously advantageous.

Incorporation of a blog on websites is a popular trend among businesses. A website is often viewed as a serious, and somewhat formal tool for communication by some customers. A blog is informal, allowing for more direct information and posts on stories that touch on what the business is looking to accomplish. At the same time, a blog allows the business to create and post fresh content periodically to boost their SEO and readership. With interesting and quality content, a website can be shared virally on social media, allowing more people to notice them and eventually increasing traffic. When businesses express creatively, they make it easier for the customers to connect with them, eventually becoming loyal customers.

**Search Engine Optimization (SEO)**

The majority of web traffic is driven by major search engines like Google, Bing, and Yahoo. Although social media and other types of traffic can generate visitors to a website, search engines are still the main method of navigation for most internet users.

As addressed in an earlier chapter, SEO is a major driving force to push traffic towards a particular website. It is a sure technique to create awareness and traffic for the website once several aspects are put into place. It is a marketing discipline primarily focused on growing visibility of a website in organic (non-paid) search engine results. SEO encompasses both the technical and creative elements. There are many aspects to SEO, from the words on the website to the way other sites are linked to the website on the internet. Sometimes, SEO is simply a matter of making sure a website is structured in a way that search engines understand. This requires developing a comprehensive SEO strategy and infrastructure.

An SEO infrastructure will have the right URL for customers who try to search for companies using a URL, the right content on the web page, appropriate links on search engine results, and the right web page structure. SEO infrastructure points to Search Engine Optimization being much more than just having good keywords. It is more holistic and allows small businesses to reach their customers effectively from the search engines, and increases their online presence, which also means an increase in long-term profitability.

## Search Engine Marketing (SEM)

Search Engine Marketing is a form of internet marketing that involves the promotion of websites by increasing their visibility on search engines. Unlike SEO, this technique is done primarily through paid advertising. Google AdWords is the most popular advertising system used by search marketers for paid advertising on Google, followed by Bing Ads, which also serves a significant portion of advertisements on Yahoo.

With millions of businesses out there, all vying for the same eyeballs on search results, it has never been more important to advertise online via paid advertising. As covered in one of the chapters, AdWords provides several customization options for businesses to target their audience effectively. At the same time, it provides businesses, big or small, a levelled playing field. One of the most enduring misconceptions about SEM is that businesses with the largest advertising budget win. However, the fact is that, although a larger advertising budget can certainly be advantageous, it is far from a requirement for success with SEM. With the right campaign setup, businesses can succeed with SEM, even when they have a low marketing budget.

**Social Media**

A small business that is looking to leverage the power of online communities and word of mouth marketing on digital platforms will ensure that they have a presence on social networking sites. As a component of digital marketing, social media forms a building block that will lead to increased awareness and profitability. Social media is big and it will only become even bigger. If businesses are not marketing on it, they are likely to miss a large chunk of their target consumers. Just because a business should be on social media, however, does not mean that the business should be on every network. It is important to choose and nurture the right social platforms that work best for the business so that they do not spread themselves too thin.

As a product of the "Mark Zuckerberg era", it is easy to understand why people are so obsessed with social media platforms. For marketers, the potential to grow their business via these networks is endless. For users, there is the attraction of connecting with new people, sharing opinions with like-minded people, and staying in touch with old friends and colleagues. Facebook, Twitter, Pinterest, Instagram, and

## Rounding Up Digital Marketing Components

LinkedIn are some of the more popular social media networks every company, big or small, young or established, can leverage on.

*Mark Zuckerberg, CEO of Facebook*

Social media can be used to create closer interactions with consumers, allowing for discussions of issues to be resolved in real time. In addition, positive news and interesting content can also be shared with customers the moment that it is available. It can drive people towards the websites of small businesses, ensuring that there is a strong online presence. When customers are looking for information on a product or service that they need, they often use the search bar on their social networking sites, and, from there, connect with a business and build a relationship. In many instances, customers discover new businesses via their newsfeed or walls from their friends or friends of friends.

Social media also provides a new channel for businesses to utilize paid advertising to reach out to more customers, and increases the reach of their marketing message. Online campaigns can also be carried out on social media to engage users actively on the social networks.

In a nutshell, social media provides businesses a platform to build its online community. It also provides a channel between brands and customers to communicate on, which is something traditional advertising will never achieve.

**Email Marketing**

Email is an incredibly powerful marketing channel. It may likely be the genesis of digital marketing efforts, and this technique still retains its significance to this day. There are several advantages of email marketing that make it relevant to digital marketing as a whole.

Firstly, this type of marketing is very direct, reaching the desired consumer in the most straightforward way possible. Most consumers nowadays are very savvy and connected. They can check their emails almost anytime and anywhere. Therefore, email makes it possible to reach them at the micro-moments. Secondly, according to research by McKinsey & Company, email marketing is 40 times more effective at attracting new business than Facebook and Twitter combined. This is because prospects who land on a website through email are more likely to convert. Thirdly, email marketing is affordable, with little-associated costs apart from the time and effort needed to collect the mailing list, and the costs of designing and developing a great email. Fourth, data can be collected from the emails sent, and businesses can analyze the data gathered to make data-driven decisions for their next marketing campaign. They can also identify consumers that are engaging with their emails and the content that interests their target consumers most. In this way, small businesses can understand their target consumers, feeding them with relevant and engaging information.

This marketing technique is not just sending out emails to consumers. There are a few factors that must be considered to contribute to its long-term success. Email marketers must ensure the subject line is information-rich and captivating, such that the prospects will be more likely to open the email to read it. At the same time, businesses must ensure that they have a clear objective for the email so the email is crafted with the correct theme and content. Due to prolific spamming, people are very protective of their email inboxes. When they feel violated or spammed, email recipients are quick to unsubscribe from mailing lists, or to flag emails as spam. That is why it is important for businesses to build their email database organically with an opt-in form on their website, blogs, podcasts or registration forms. The power of images and visual stimulants should also not be underestimated. It will make content more engaging and relevant to the email subscribers.

With the power of data, email segmentation can be done in a way that businesses can strategically target their message: sending out different emails based on the content that prospects view and download on the website, the information they provide via the call-to-action, and other relevant data.

Creating winning email marketing will result in a net increase in lead generation and sales with each round of emails in the short run. Although it may be tempting, refrain from emailing too often, thus wearing out the goodwill, or risk portraying the emails as spam.

### Rocket Into Digital

The email is alive and kicking, but the modern consumer is savvier and more protective of their inbox than ever. With minimal efforts, email marketers can keep audiences engaged and convert them. The inbox could very well become the place where consumers interact with the brands that reach them.

*EDM by Tesla Motors on Model S*

## Content Marketing

Content marketing is essential to digital marketing since it is the fuel that powers all digital marketing channels from search, social and email marketing. It is vital for increasing lead and sale conversion rates. Content marketing is an umbrella term covering several strategies, techniques, and tactics that can be used to fulfil the business' and customers' goals by serving relevant content to attract, convert, retain and engage customers. It is used across the customer journey, customer life cycle, and looks at the customer from a connected perspective.

One of the aims of content marketing is to optimize business value and customer value, providing and enabling the right content across the right channels in the most timely, valuable, connected, personalized and optimized way, across (and beyond) the audience life cycle. Without proper planning, using several social networking sites and digital platforms can result in a message that is not cohesive. Therefore, for content marketing to be carried out, the small business marketer will need to create a content calendar. In this calendar, all the communication campaigns taking place against all digital platforms will be written down in detail. In this way, it is easy to assess what messages are being sent out and to gauge whether all the messages are related to each other.

A content calendar also allows for the effective planning of any information that is to be sent out to customers. As digital marketing happens in real time, there is a possibility of misinformation, especially when one is faced with pressure from time. A content calendar helps to control what information trickles down to the customer, and who is in charge of sending out that information.

Content marketing in digital marketing contributes to driving conversions through the number of visitors to a website, and the level at which these visitors are engaged. Every small business that is marketing digitally should ensure that the content available on their website is current, attractive, and result oriented.

Thought leadership strategy is a standard component of content marketing - and for good reason. A successful content strategy always brings new insight to customers. The content must be valuable by educating or informing the audience on a deeper level. To meet this criterion, content should be of exceptional quality, and should engage the customer. There should be interesting headlines to encourage more clicks on the site, and, where necessary, information should be repurposed so that it appears to be more current. Further, there should be visually appealing components to content online, rather than simple text. Visual representation makes it easier for a customer to relate to a product or service, and also makes a site more attractive.

Content can be pushed on a website through blog use, particularly if it centers on offering helpful advice and information to customers. The key to getting content marketing right on a digital platform is to always approach it with a strategy in mind.

Rome was not built in a day, and its buildings still stand. A good content marketer should retain great content longer if it is optimized and resonates with the audience. He/she should tear down and rebuild recent content that is not working. Content marketing is a strategy that takes time and effort to build. However, the result can be rewarding for most businesses.

## A to Z of Content Marketing

These tips outline the basics of promoting and creating content to help maximize reach and return for a business' efforts.

A - Submit the blog to **AllTop.com**: get a "DoFollow" link and ongoing traffic, too, if the content is good.

B - **Bookmark** blog posts. Find sites in the industry where experts hang out.
- Growthhackers.com - Growth Hacking
- Inbound.org - Inbound Marketing
- SocialMediaToday.com - Digital Marketing

C - **Curate** content. This generation is all about content curation. They like to Scoop & Flip stories.
- Scoop.it
- Storify
- Flipboard

D - Submit to **Digg & Delicious**: worth adding to the content marketing list and experimenting.

E - **Email** the list. Build an email list and maintain a relationship with them. Recurring traffic will come from this list.

F - **Facebook** & Facebook Groups: Build an online community.

G - **Google+** & G+ Communities.

H - Check the competitors' **History**. If one is looking for more social reach, then check out which influencers have shared the competitors' content and then reach out to them with better content. One can also do the same by checking out their competitors' backlink history.

I - **Influencer Marketing**. Tap on influencers to multiply the content reach. Influencers can significantly increase reach and thus save time.

J - Be a Content Marketing **Joe**, always keep learning. Content marketing is not a set and forget strategy. One has to follow a checklist and constantly keep updating it. New platforms will come in, and old platforms will phase out.

K - Content is **King** and the use of keywords. Content quality is like ground zero: regardless of the content marketing effort or budget, if the content quality is poor then the results will not be good. Search engine traffic is one of the best ongoing promotional techniques, and it starts with keywords.

L - **LinkedIn & Groups**. Use LinkedIn as a professional network to spread awesome content.

M - Post on **Medium**. Medium is a content marketing paradise and use it wisely. It is easy to use, free of cost, and has a built-in audience, thus giving businesses content creation and promotion all in one place.

N - Use the **News**. Use the news headlines and release dates of interesting launches to produce content.

O - **Opportunity**. Always be on the lookout for content

## Rounding Up Digital Marketing Components

creation ideas and marketing opportunities.

P - **Pinterest** and Collaborator Boards. Create visually stunning content and pin them. Join group boards where business can collaborate and pin. The more followers a group board has, the better.

Q - **Quora.** Use Quora to showcase expertise and knowledge.

R - **Reddit & Roundups.** Find an appropriate sub-reddit and submit content. Search for roundups for topics on Google.

S - **StumbleUpon & Syndicated Content.** Organic Stumbles can work wonders and bring in viral traffic without much additional effort, unlike other social media sites.

T - Using **Twitter** is a must. Use images and hashtags to amplify content reach.

U - Focus on **User Experience** (UX): Content with no experience is more like a newspaper. Anyone can provide great content, but not everyone can bundle it with great UX.

V- **Videos**, Infographics, and SlideShare Presentations should be used to create appealing content.

W - **Work** for it and help others share awesome content.

X - **Expand** the horizon. Do not just write on one blog. Write as a guest blogger on industry sites to spread the brand name and content.

Y - **Your X Factor.** Market content with flare. What is the business good at? How can one use their personality?

Z - Last but not least: **Zest up the content with Paid Traffic and Leveraging Personal Relationships**.

## Video Marketing

When it comes to digital marketing, the role of video is becoming increasingly evident. Today, more than ever, businesses realize that video has a vital role to play in the digital marketing strategy. It is a valuable tool for capturing the audience's attention and delivering a brand message in a memorable and meaningful way. It is an easy, shareable way to communicate a business' core message. Videos drive results, and with the inclusion of analytics and reports, small businesses can track results more effectively to learn which videos or assets are responsible for the most return on investments.

*Video campaign from Mullen and Cardstore by American Greetings #WorldsToughestJob*

With online video rapidly becoming a key means for people to satisfy their thirst for information and entertainment needs, small businesses that fail to include this strategy in their digital marketing plan will do so at their peril. When it comes to the potential outreach, video marketing is excellent. YouTube receives more than one billion unique visitors every month - that is more than any other channel, apart from Facebook.

Small businesses can engage viewers via videos, and these viewers will then share the video with others. They will also spend more time on the website, interacting with the brand. For any social media campaign, video marketing is without a doubt one of the best tools in the kit. If a picture paints 1,000 words, then a one minute of video is worth 1.8 million words.

## Mobile Marketing

Mobile marketing is massive already and expected to exceed desktop internet access in many countries. While sitting at home, it is far easier to research a product one has seen on television via a smartphone than it is to fire up a desktop computer and wait minutes for it to boot up.

Therefore, every marketer needs to keep tabs on the opportunities available to reach their target audiences via mobile, and how to make their website presence visible and accessible through mobile devices. It involves communicating with the consumer via the mobile device: either to send a marketing message, to introduce them to a new campaign, or to allow them to visit a mobile-friendly website.

Mobile marketing provides the opportunity for any-time, any-place, anywhere connection to the audience. During the early

2000s, mobile marketing became familiar with the use of text messaging in Europe and parts of Asia. Subsequently, SMS marketing has become a legitimate advertising channel in both developed and developing economies around the world. Today, the inception of multiple mobile devices have transformed digital marketing because they open up radically new touchpoints for where and when businesses can connect to their customers with more than 40% of online adults using multi-devices. Mobile marketing promotional tactics have since evolved to include push notifications, QR codes, keyword advertising and mobile game marketing.

Push notifications have become increasingly more popular due to their use on smart devices running iOS and Android operating systems. These notifications appear at the top of the device's screen and serve as efficient mechanisms for communicating directly with end-users. This function allows businesses to serve users the latest promotions and key marketing messages, to engage their target audience, and to convert them.

With the surge of mobile gaming activities, mobile game marketing has also become a popular marketing channel for businesses to leverage on. It provides additional opportunities for brands looking to deliver promotional messaging within mobile games. Some companies even sponsor the entire games to drive consumer engagement, a practice known as mobile advergaming or ad-funded mobile gaming.

It is necessary for all businesses to keep the online journey as fluid and consistent as possible for customers. Regardless of the industry, mobile marketing will continue to play a vital role in the customer purchase journey or lifecycle.

"If you have more money than brains, you should focus on outbound marketing. If you have more brains than money, you should focus on inbound marketing."

- Guy Kawasaki (Former Chief Evangelist, Apple)

**Rocket Into Digital**

# Chapter 8

# Gaining the Vivid Competitive Edge

Digital marketing is just as cluttered as traditional marketing. Understanding how to gain the competitive edge on digital platforms is a science, it requires intensive understanding and methodology, as well as a proper strategy to meet goals. There are certain steps that small businesses can take to be more competitive while leveraging digital marketing.

**Build**

Digital marketing and social media are meant to engage a customer so that they can eventually make a purchase of a product or a service. This is not a relationship that occurs automatically: it is one that has to be built.

That is where content comes into play. Social networking pages can be boring and forgotten, unless they have relevant, fresh content as often as possible, that the customer can relate to. The more people interact and communicate with a small business on a social media platform, the easier it becomes for that business to develop a relationship as well as to engage with the customers.

This relationship makes the customers feel that they are important, rather than leaving them feeling that they are just a statistic, or a means to an end. Social Media offers small businesses a digital megaphone for communication. With such an excellent tool, it is vital that the communication pitches the business above all the rest.

## Evolve

Digital marketing is not static, and companies that do not change their approach or advertisements periodically risk disappearing into the background and being beaten by the competition. It is, therefore, crucial for marketing messages on digital platforms to evolve. This evolution is what creates differentiation and retains customer interest.

By evolving, small businesses are also able to showcase how they stay ahead of the competition by exhibiting leadership through innovation. This can easily be seen by updating websites to fresh designs after a period, and finding new avenues for customer engagement. A small business may have started out with just a website, and over the duration of a year, included a host of social networking platforms that customers can access through the website. Businesses that fail to evolve on digital platforms risk expiring and being completely irrelevant in the market.

## Learn

To retain a competitive advantage on digital platforms, it is necessary to be aware of what is happening within the industry.

Information on digital channels should be accurate and relevant so that the customer gets a clear picture of the product and the industry.

To get this type of information, particularly in a fast-moving industry, a small business marketer should read information from blogs and articles that offer similar products or services. This will make it easier to identify new trends and come up with strategies that will help stay ahead of the competition.

There are also a significant number of conferences that are taking place all over the world, focusing on digital marketing and social media optimization. Small businesses should attend, and, where possible, participate so that they can learn about how to craft effective campaigns. These events help provide valuable tools, some of which are not discussed elsewhere.

The small business marketer should scour the internet for new technologies, and then adopt those that can help improve their digital marketing strategy. As there are so many available, there should be some freedom in experimenting with different channels to find out through experience which one would be the best fit for the business.

## Participate

There are ways that small business can encourage participation from their clientele on digital marketing and social media channels, and this involvement can indeed provide the sought after competitive edge. One way is through creating engaging contests, where participants are encouraged to create blog posts about an interaction with the product, and a forum or social media platform allowing for comments that help gather feedback from customers.

Contests will motivate the average customer to interact with the product and take part in the competition, especially as they often have prizes that can be won in the end. A well-executed contest also has the added advantage of creating a sensational buzz, which is sure to propel the small business to greater heights.

## Giveaway

This is an old, but useful, technique of encouraging customer engagement and gaining a competitive edge. It requires giving away the product or service to customers to encourage them to try it and then purchase it. How it works is to offer a limited number of clients a deal that seems too good to be true - but that is actually true.

What should happen is that many people should sign up on the online platform to try the product or service, or to get a chance to win. As well as creating a sense of excitement, particularly if the competition is doing nothing similar, this technique also ensures that the small business can build up a sizeable database.

Giveaways should last for a short period to be effective, such as three months. In this time, independent bloggers may also take the time to share information on the giveaway, creating an opportunity to reach an even wider customer base.

## Interact

Social media allows for real-time interactions between small business and its audience. This goes a long way in improving

## Gaining the Vivid Competitive Edge

customer service. Websites, where customers can digitally interact with their customers, have a sure competitive edge over others that do not have this capability.

Interaction is important, especially since most people are connected to the internet 24 hours a day, thanks to their mobile devices. When it comes to communication, small businesses should have one target: to be the first to implement anything and to interact in any way with the customers. The competitive advantage is that all the other competitors will spend their time playing catch-up, instead of formulating new campaigns that they can execute themselves.

### Spread

For an excellent competitive edge, the digital marketing and social media approach should be spread out. This means that no single channel should bear the weight of social marketing, but rather should be spread over all the other digital marketing channels. There should be a website, and supporting this website should be platforms on social networks.

There should also be pay per click advertising options available, as noted in the previous chapter on Google AdWords, as an example. This is something that financial experts do: they avoid putting all their eggs in one basket. This is a mentality that will also serve the digital marketer well.

### Visibility

Years ago, when digital marketing was first introduced, to be visible online meant to have large fonts, perhaps some music playing in the background when one sends a message, and also have some small pictures on the website, which more often than not, blended into the background discretely.

Today, there are various ways that a digital marketer can increase visibility online to retain the competitive edge. The latest method being used requires incorporating video on a website, which is a good way to draw the attention of the consumer and relay a message that they are more likely to remember.

Increasing visibility does not automatically translate into sales, but it does improve the competitive advantage. People are likely to spend more time on websites that offer visual stimulation than they are on sites that have continuous prose.

## Focus

It can be tempting to create broad marketing messages, or try to reach all the different types of online consumers possible through a digital marketing campaign. A keen marketer may attempt to tailor-make a range of messages, and to push these forward on multiple channels. To remain interactive and relevant, and in an attempt to beat the competition, some small business marketers will bombard their customers with messages.

To retain a competitive advantage, the small business marketer needs to maintain their focus. Focus means understanding the outcome that they want to achieve from digital marketing efforts, and the strategy that should be followed to meet that outcome.

Rather than there being a volume of information, there should

**Gaining the Vivid Competitive Edge**

be clarity in communication. This means that what may sound like a sales pitch should be eliminated, as digital marketing uses a pull-method rather than a push-strategy when communicating with the customer.

**Rocket Into Digital**

"Create content that teaches. You can't give up. You need to be consistently awesome."

- Neil Patel (Co-Founder, Crazy Egg and KISSmetrics)

**Rocket Into Digital**

# Chapter 9

# Bridging the Distance Gap and Maintaining Customer Closeness

Many people have archaic memories and references to digital marketing and its effectiveness. The most defined idea around digital marketing, from a negative perspective, is the use or abuse of email marketing. As long as one has an email address, he/she may have already fallen prey to marketers who send junk email. Junk mail refers to an email that contains marketing messages sent out to thousands of people all at once.

The result is that this type of messaging is a generic message that does not in any way help to build customer loyalty. If anything, a customer can even feel insulted, and is likely to take one main action: that is to delete the offensive message.

There are also email marketing messages that contain too much marketing information, so much so that when a customer receives these messages they are overwhelmed and unlikely to read the entire message. Instead, they move quickly towards the delete button yet again.

Digital marketing requires a delicate balance, and in this

balance, it is important for the small business marketer to understand what steps need to be taken to establish and maintain customer closeness, for the development of long-term relationships.

## Discerning Customer Perceptions and Identifying their Needs

Perception is reality. This is important for a marketer to remember, because it is highly possible that a customer's perception of a product may be flawed, but as long as that is the way that they view the product, that is also the direction the marketer should take. Communication needs to meet the perceptions of the customer to encourage closeness and growth of the products.

How does a marketer get the right information on customer perceptions to ensure that their digital marketing efforts are encouraging consumer closeness? The answer lies in conducting polls and surveys and getting direct feedback from the customers. This can be done through email or social networks, as they provide raw and relevant data.

Once a marketer has a clear idea of customer perceptions, it becomes possible to identify the customers' needs. By doing so, a digital marketer can then ensure that there is targeted information reaching the right customers.

To round off the building of customer relationships, digital marketers need to collect feedback from the customers, so that they can find out whether their communication is effective. This is the way that they can gauge customer satisfaction.

## Integrating Digital Marketing Channels

So far, there are several channels that have been identified for effective digital marketing. These include search engines, social networks and even email marketing. All these media are used to reach customers, giving them information on the product or addressing their needs. In order to build closeness, these should also be integrated. One can quickly and efficiently lead to the other. Take, for example, an email marketing message. There should be a link in that message that directs someone to the company's website. Once on the website, it should be possible to connect to the social networking platforms. This helps a customer identify what is most convenient for them, in terms of getting information about the company and its products.

Small businesses must ensure that all their digital channels are employed adequately for there to be excellent customer closeness. This is a strategy that is sure to amass a significant amount of customers, all ensuring that they have access to information on the products as, and when, they need it.

## Digital Marketing Should Make a Difference

People are looking for information and products that will add value and enrich their lives. A business may have a product that can do exactly this, but without the right communication on digital platforms, the product will have no sales.

To communicate how a product can make a difference, by analyzing the marketing message, a story can be told. The objective of telling a story is to induce some emotional closeness between the marketing message and the customers. This will not only increase the customer closeness, it can have a surprising positive effect on competitive advantage.

## Engage the Customer

The customers need to be able to communicate with the small business, by sharing their ideas about the products or services that are on offer. When a customer is comfortable enough to do this, there is an excellent opportunity to build up good customer relationships and ensure customer satisfaction.

For this reason, every digital channel that is used should have a section where the customers can give some feedback or send a message. When these messages appear publicly, other customers can find out new benefits of using the product and are more likely to also want to create a connection.

Some small businesses have the relevant concern that opening up digital platforms in this way can result in a loss of business, particularly if there is a bad review. This scenario actually presents an excellent opportunity for digital marketers. They can show their customer development skills by publicly addressing all complaints and ensuring that customers reach a point of satisfaction. This goes a long way in developing customer closeness and ensuring long-term loyalty.

## Business Transparency

Customers are more likely to feel close to the company if they can connect with the management in order to voice their concerns about the products and services. For a small business this is not only essential, it is also practical. Customers feel they can trust a business when they receive responses from management in regards to observations, complaints and compliments.

This creates a deep emotional connection, one which would be enthusiastically communicated using word of mouth to other customers. Being transparent in communication and processes can lead to customers wanting to engage more often with the small business. An essential way a small business can create transparency is through email marketing. When sending out a message, the picture of the executive can be used as part of the marketing message so that the consumers have an idea of who they are interacting with. This helps put a voice to the message and makes it feel as though there is someone they can see, connect with and get feedback from.

Customers are more likely to trust this sort of information than they are to trust a company that appears to be faceless. When a recipient sees a headshot, the small business is communicating that this is someone that can be trusted, without having to explicitly convey those words. Being transparent is an excellent way to build up sales and customer loyalty.

## Being Accountable

Digital marketing and social media present small businesses the opportunity to be accountable for their actions – the way they do business and the products that they sell. By opening up a direct communication platform with customers, small businesses can explain when things go wrong, inform when things go right, and encourage their customers to continue engaging with them.

Being accountable also trickles down into ensuring that

excellent products and services are provided with the aim of building better customer service. Any organization on a digital platform that offers exceptional customer service is also likely to have a strong and loyal customer base.

## Social Responsibility

Customers may feel separated from a company if there is evidence that the company is not socially responsible. There are websites that try to exhibit that they are socially responsible in their digital marketing efforts. This includes providing disclaimers on age appropriateness, expected customers, and step-by-step processes for attaining a goal.

Digital marketers may also find themselves in a position where they have to support a cause in order to please their customers and to retain them in the competitive atmosphere. This builds excellent brand equity.

When customers feel close to the small business due to social responsibility, they are likely to accelerate the momentum of these campaigns, and cause a viral message while digital marketing campaigns are taking place.

## Build a Personal Relationship

Digital marketing messages can be quite informal, leading a customer to believe that they are not relevant to the small business. However, by building a personal relationship with a customer, this distance gap can easily be overcome.

Take, for example, email marketing. Digital marketing efforts should be very targeted, meaning that marketers should ensure

## Bridging the Distance Gap and Maintaining Customer Closeness

they have adequately segmented their mailing lists. This should be followed by personalization. Rather than the heading of an email saying something like "Dear Customer", it should address the recipient by name. This way, it appears that there is a personal connection with the customer.

Email marketing messages should also have a personal tone. One would speak differently in a face-to-face conversation when dealing with a business executive and when dealing with a friend. When sending out digital messages, they should have the tone that one would have used when they were talking things over with a friend. Words like "me" and "you" are more personal than words like "they". The exception to this rule is when one is dealing with a very formal market.

As a digital marketer, it is important to remember that digital marketing can be a technical process, where one has to follow certain steps and at the end of it all, attain some positive result. This can be evident in increased sales or more customer interaction. The challenge that marketers have is maintaining these relationships over an extended period.

To ensure that there is customer closeness for the long term, small businesses must take the time to focus on digital marketing. They can do so by having a person who is dedicated to managing the digital marketing platforms. This person will spend each day actively engaging with customers online through social networks, and will answer their enquiries and give feedback.

The dedicated employee will also take the time to update all digital marketing channels as often as possible. By having this person in place, it becomes much easier to drive sales and change basic interactions into conversions. It also allows the small business brand to have a human face, making it easier to connect with the customers and to develop a relationship with them.

Businesses, for the most part, are quite serious in their communication, but with digital marketing, companies should take the opportunity to inject some humor into their interaction with customers. Customers enjoy having something to smile about and are more likely to develop relationships with sites where they feel good while they interact. In addition to posts giving information about products, and those which handle customer queries, small businesses can include thoughtful quotes, humorous jokes and inspirational messages on their digital platforms (especially social networks), when they are engaging with their customers. Customers are likely to share, and the ultimate result could easily be even more customers.

"Marketing without data is like driving with your eyes closed."

- Dan Zarrella (Social Media Scientist, HubSpot)

**Rocket Into Digital**

# Conclusion

Digital marketing is without a doubt the way forward for many small businesses. The overall market is highly competitive, and businesses are forced to come up with strategies that make them relevant and up-to-date. Digital marketing has been proven to present a significant amount of value-added benefits for small businesses.

These include allowing a wider marketing reach to targeted customers. Unlike traditional marketing, where a billboard is accessible to every person in the vicinity, a digital ad can be created to reach a specific demographic only, leading to an increased possibility of sales.

This book has also revealed that small businesses that are interested in improving their bottom line should consider digital marketing. There are so many channels that can be used to attain business growth. All that is required is to have the right message, a properly segmented market, and the time to create an interesting and engaging campaign. When a digital marketing strategy is well put together, it can result in sales growth by up to 300%.

Effective use of social media can also lead to a considerable competitive edge. This is critical for small businesses as they are competing with a large number of other entities online, both big and small. Having the edge could be the difference between staying afloat or not surviving.

This book explains why social media is so important for the small business and the different social networks that one can capitalize on to build a brand. It is important to remember that each social network serves its own purpose, and, therefore, digital marketers should avoid creating generic messages that they place across all platforms. It would be ideal to have a particular message that is tailored towards each platform, so that there can be maximization of customer engagement.

Overall, digital marketing and social media was the way to the future a decade ago and is the way of successfully operating a business now. Since this marketing can reach people on their personal computers and laptops, as well as their mobile devices, it has substantial reach and influence over customer behavior.

Small businesses should ensure that they understand everything possible about digital marketing, from the artistic point of view where they put together attractive messages to engage a customer, to the scientific point of view, where methodology and strategy come into play. By discerning the art and science of this communication, a small business will grow their customer base and increase sales.

"If consumers can be on any channel, brands need to be on every channel."

- Vincent Wee (Digital Marketer and Author)

**Rocket Into Digital**

# About the Author

Vincent is a dynamic and versatile marketing strategist primarily focused in the digital marketing industry. With experience spanning several positions from Co-Founder of a successful tech-startup to Digital Marketing Director at a prestigious media-accredited creative agency. He has habitually proven his diligence and ability to creatively solve problems both in a team setting and individually. In his 9+ years of professional experience he has also successfully published several informative articles widely read by marketers worldwide as well as mastering the art of design and development.

Using a creative yet systematic approach to develop powerful marketing strategies he has helped hundreds of businesses to boost sales, build brand awareness, and successfully increase market presence. His ability to concoct these effective strategies comes from his versatile background, having worked in engineering, interior design, marketing and creative industries. These efforts usually result in a lucrative, long lasting relationship and raving recommendations from the clients specifically due to his excellent project management and inter-personal skills.

Vincent enjoys traveling and collecting designer novelties such as Gunpla (ガンプラ), but he's particularly passionate about an intense and team-centered multiplayer game called DOTA 2. Success in this game requires sharp critical thinking skills and an even better ability to execute a collaborative strategy. His superior ability to conquer opponents in this game undoubtedly corresponds with his ability to strategize and work collaboratively in a professional setting.

Daily Focus:
"Attitude is a little thing that makes a big difference."


Visit my website: http://www.VincentWee.com/

# Thank You For Your Support!

www.ingramcontent.com/pod-product-compliance
Lightning Source LLC
Chambersburg PA
CBHW060900170526
45158CB00001B/432